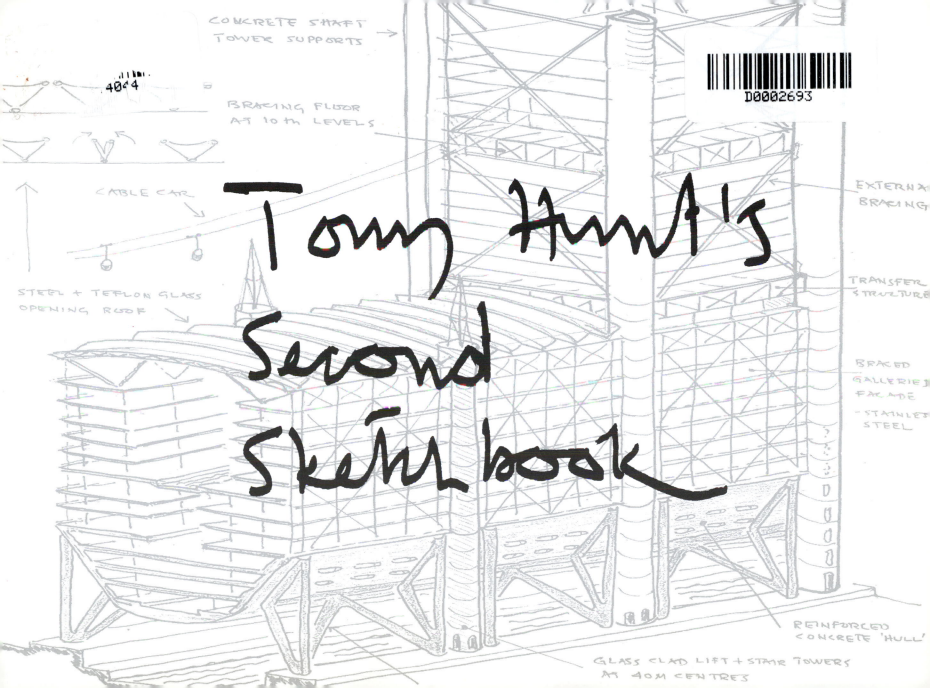

Architectural Press
An imprint of Elsevier Science
Linacre House, Jordan Hill, Oxford OX2 8DP
200 Wheeler Road, Burlington, MA 01803

First published 1999
Second edition 2003

British Library Cataloguing in Publication Data
A catalogue record for this book is available from the British Library

Library of Congress Cataloguing in Publication Data
A catalogue record for this book is available from the Library of Congress

ISBN 0 7506 5896 7

For information on all Architectural Press publications
visit our website at www.architecturalpress.com

Typeset by Genesis Typesetting Ltd
Printed and bound in Great Britain by Martins-the-Printers, Berwick-upon-Tweed

To Diana

Architectural Press
OXFORD   AMSTERDAM   BOSTON   LONDON   NEW YORK   PARIS   SAN DIEGO
SAN FRANCISCO   SINGAPORE   SYDNEY   TOKYO
http://www.architecturalpress.com

Contents

Preface to the First Book of Sketches

Drawing to me is an essential delight – I don't feel comfortable thinking about a design problem without a pencil in my hand.

As a young engineer I discovered that describing a structural concept or detail wasn't very effective unless illustrated with a sketch to explain my ideas. My mind has the ideas but they only become 'real' through the medium of sketching, since mental ideas, as yet, cannot be transmitted to others. And anyway, the act of drawing what the mind 'sees' generates a design or detail, good or not so good, which immediately leads to alternatives.

So, besides being a delight early design sketches, sometimes very rough, are my way of imparting overall concepts and details to other members of the design team for discussion and modification.

I hope that readers of this sketchbook will be encouraged to do as I have always done – to draw their ideas as a first means of imparting their design ideas to others.

Tony Hunt

Preface to the Second Book of Sketches

Since writing the preface for my sketchbook, I have, of course, been involved in a number of more recent projects where I have sketched ideas for structural solutions.

In addition, looking through my archive of drawings I have discovered some early work which I have included in this second edition as I think that it will be of interest to show the progression of my drawing style and differing structural approaches over the years.

Despite the almost universal use today of CAD (computer-aided drawing), which always gives the impression of a finite final solution, I strongly believe that during the initial phase of any design, hand-drawn sketches are still the best form of communication.

I hope that this second edition will inspire young and not so young designers to keep drawing.

Carlo Scarpa the famous Italian designer said: 'I draw because I want to see'.

Tony Hunt

Introduction to the First Book of Sketches by Sir Norman Foster

From my earliest recollections as a student of architecture I remember being fascinated by how buildings were made and being equally frustrated by not having that knowledge at my fingertips. How, I wondered, could you ever start to design a building without knowing what made it stand up? Then, as now, I still find it a contradiction that in so many schools of architecture the means of construction can be divorced from the process of design, to the point of it being considered an unfashionable tedium.

At Manchester University I remember knocking on the door of the structures lecturer and trying to engage him in a conversation about my design project. It was an uphill task because this engineer, like most of his profession, was used to being handed a design already conceived by an architect. He saw his role as one of amending the concept so that enough structure could be inserted to enable it to stand up, regardless of any wider implications. In a teaching environment it would follow that structures could only be considered in the abstract.

Repeat the same pattern with the engineers responsible for the environmental systems in a building and the design process could be described as a game of 'passing the parcel'. Eventually, the drawings are shuttled to and fro enough times to achieve the desired level of co-ordination. Maybe I exaggerate a little to make the point. However, the reality is that most engineers in this field see their task as a passive one – whether by education, attitude or prevailing practice. Tony Hunt is a refreshing exception to this pattern and I will try to explain why.

The best design solutions in any field are about integration – about dissolving the traditional boundaries between the systems and component parts which make up artifacts and buildings alike. In architecture this could mean a structure which is doing much more than simply holding the building aloft. It may be conceived as an important element in the ecology of the building, through thermal mass or the means of distributing air, light, energy or services.

Issues of prefabrication will also influence the weight, materials, appearance and the methods of production. Structure can also be manipulated to the extent that it becomes the architecture – the means of defining interior spaces and exterior volume – the structural form becomes the emblematic image. Or perhaps the structure does not have its own identity, maybe it dissolves into the form in the manner of the monocoque shells of aircraft and boats.

The possibilities are endless. But the starting point is a creative process in which the engineer participates actively from the outset, alongside the other individuals who share knowledge and responsibility. This demands an awareness of wider issues beyond the limits of specialist knowledge, the ability to 'change hats' with those other specialists who service, cost and build buildings. When the respect and sense of values is shared by a dynamic group, then it is possible to challenge the status quo and even, on occasions, to innovate.

Individuals who can share the spirit of such endeavours are rare in any profession. Tony Hunt, structural engineer par excellence, is one. It is an important part of the answer to why he has amassed such a wide range of impressive structures. One of his great strengths is that he does not come to any design session with preconceptions – he is open to consider options, but if pressed for an opinion then he will always be articulate and not only verbally.

Communication is an essential part of the creative process and Tony Hunt is a master of the encapsulating sketch. I dearly wish that his sketchbooks and his inspiration had been available to me when I was a student struggling to understand about structure. Tony Hunt's brilliance shines through these pages and it is a privilege to share his insights through these notes and images.

Introduction to the Second Book of Sketches by Michael Manser

Tony Hunt has one of the most fertile minds in the building industry. For over thirty years he has provided the structural engineering for a high proportion of the most inventive architecture by its most distinguished practitioners. More than almost any other individual, he has moved the role of structural engineering from that of a passive support for an architectural design already determined to being an active and key participant in its earliest sketches.

Small, energetic and quick, his alert eyes and hands seem to work as one to make the sketches shown in this book. Each session with him, as an architectural and structural design evolves, is also like a lecture on the elegance of the tension and compressive forces which he seems to see in space like a three-dimensional musical score. To take an early sketch idea of a building of any sort to Tony is to come away with a better piece of architecture.

He is an instinctive communicator to the architects with whom he works, and to the engineers in his relaxed and democratic office. More formally, he has for many years taught students in university schools of architecture and engineering. His enthusiasm and utter pleasure in his work, which he offers in equal measure of scholarship and humour, commands vigorous responses from clients and colleagues in his design team, as well as from students at all stages of their courses.

This is his second book of sketches. Both reflect his temperament and intellect, being spare in words, with clear, explicit ideas and sketches of simple, original and precise engineering.

Several generations of architects owe much of the success of their buildings to collaborations with Tony Hunt. Several generations of young engineers have now passed through his offices, and learned more than they did at university, and some have started their own engineers' offices, spreading his influence and ethos to yet more young engineers. All architects and structural engineers and students should have this sketch book. They tell so much more about the excitement, pleasure and importance of structural engineering than many a worthy academic tome or textbook. They also teach something of the business of engineering, and how to present complicated techniques to clients and colleagues in a readily digestible format.

US Embassy

London

Job: US Embassy, London

Client: US Government

Architect: Eero Saarinen/YRM

Date: 1957–1959 – Built

- Design sketches to illustrate all the precast concrete elements of the superstructure above first floor level
- The perimeter structure is made up of 'O' frame precast units with linking top and bottom units
- The long span floors consist of precast/prestressed beam units with precast *troughs* spanning between them and an in situ concrete topping

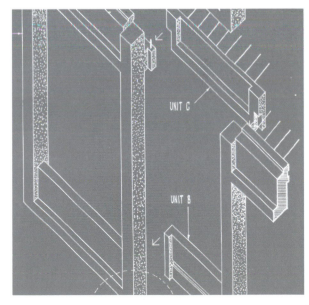

US Embassy, London

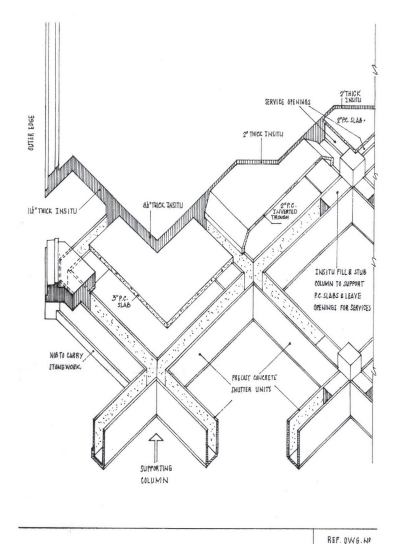

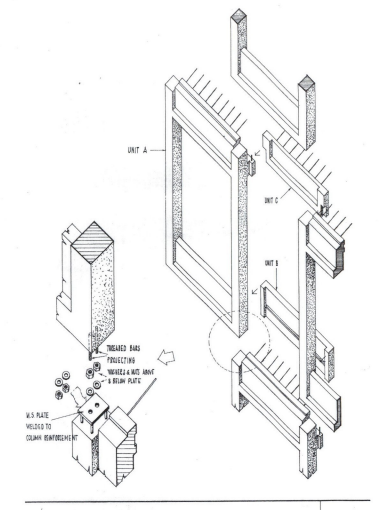

SERVICE OPENINGS

2" THICK INSITU

2" P.C. SLAB

2" THICK INSITU

OUTER EDGE

11½" THICK INSITU

8½" THICK INSITU

2" P.C. INVERTED TROUGH

INSITU FILL & STUB COLUMN TO SUPPORT P.C. SLABS & LEAVE OPENINGS FOR SERVICES

3" P.C. SLAB

NIB TO CARRY STONEWORK.

PRECAST CONCRETE SHUTTER UNITS

SUPPORTING COLUMN

UNIT A

UNIT C

UNIT B

THREADED BARS PROJECTING

WASHERS & NUTS ABOVE & BELOW PLATE

M.S. PLATE WELDED TO COLUMN REINFORCEMENT

SCHEMATIC VIEW OF DIAGRID FLOOR
SHOWING METHOD OF CONSTRUCTION

REF. DWG. Nº

1

EXPLODED VIEW OF PRECAST CONCRETE 'O' FRAMES

REF. DWG. Nº

7

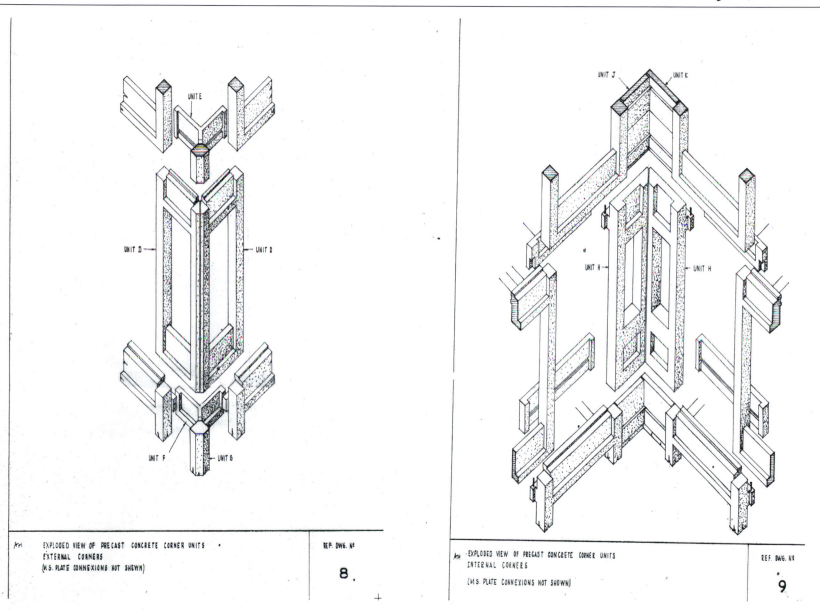

UNIT E

UNIT D — UNIT D

UNIT F — UNIT G

UNIT J — UNIT K

UNIT H — UNIT H

EXPLODED VIEW OF PRECAST CONCRETE CORNER UNITS
EXTERNAL CORNERS
(M.S. PLATE CONNEXIONS NOT SHEWN)

REF. DWG. Nº

8.

EXPLODED VIEW OF PRECAST CONCRETE CORNER UNITS
INTERNAL CORNERS
(M.S. PLATE CONNEXIONS NOT SHEWN)

REF. DWG. Nº

9

US Embassy, London

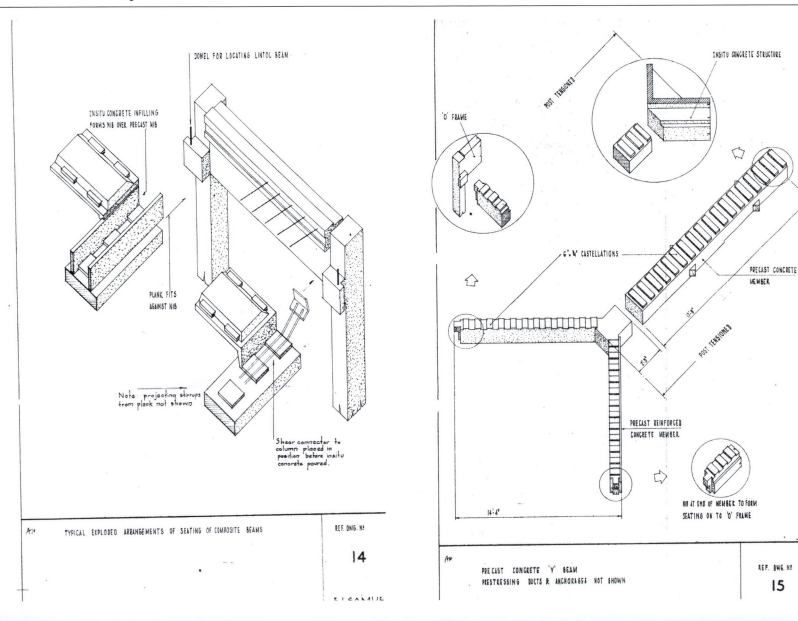

DOWEL FOR LOCATING LINTOL BEAM

INSITU CONCRETE INFILLING
FORMS NIB OVER PRECAST NIB

PLANK FITS
AGAINST NIB

Note projecting stirrups
from plank not shown

Shear connector to
column placed in
position before insitu
concrete poured.

A14   TYPICAL EXPLODED ARRANGEMENTS OF SEATING OF COMPOSITE BEAMS

REF. DWG. Nº

14

INSITU CONCRETE STRUCTURE

POST TENSIONED

'O' FRAME

6"x 4" CASTELLATIONS

PRECAST CONCRETE
MEMBER

POST TENSIONED

PRECAST REINFORCED
CONCRETE MEMBER

14'-4"

NIB AT END OF MEMBER TO FORM
SEATING ON TO 'O' FRAME

A14

PRECAST CONCRETE 'Y' BEAM
PRESTRESSING DUCTS & ANCHORAGES NOT SHOWN

REF. DWG. Nº

15

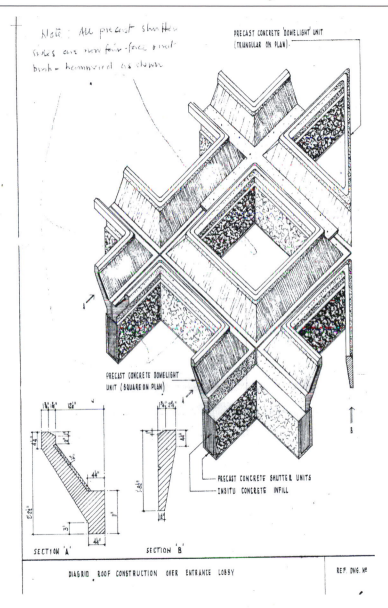

Note: All precast shutter
sides are now fair-faced and
bush-hammered as shown

PRECAST CONCRETE 'DOMELIGHT' UNIT
(TRIANGULAR ON PLAN).

PRECAST CONCRETE 'DOMELIGHT'
UNIT (SQUARE ON PLAN).

PRECAST CONCRETE SHUTTER UNITS

INSITU CONCRETE INFILL

SECTION 'A'   SECTION 'B'

DIAGRID ROOF CONSTRUCTION OVER ENTRANCE LOBBY   REF. DWG. Nº

5

Reliance Controls Factory

Job: Reliance Controls Factory, Swindon

Client: Reliance Controls

Architect: Team 4

Date: 1965 – Built

- Aim – to design a simple low cost flat roof office/assembly building
- Use 'off the shelf' standard products
- Structure using only four elements as welded steel frame:
  Column and crosshead
  Main beam
  Secondary beam
  Diagonal bracing
- Profile steel sheet cladding spans top to bottom
- Profile steel roof deck double fixed to eliminate plan bracing
- All services run through floor slab via central duct
- Designed for simple future extension
- Note: subsequently extended with minimum disruption

Reliance Controls Factory, Swindon

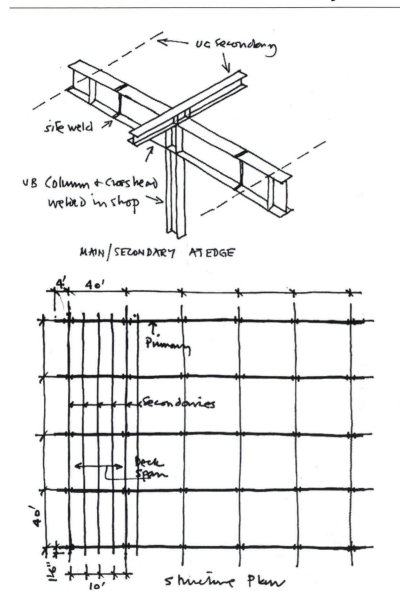

UC Secondary

site weld

UB Column + Crosshead welded in shop

MAIN / SECONDARY AT EDGE

Primary

Secondaries

Deck Span

structure Plan

4' 40'

40'

1'6"

10'

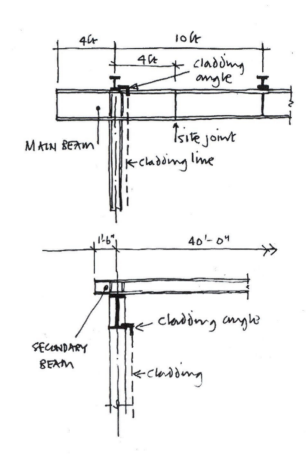

4ft 10ft

4ft cladding angle

MAIN BEAM site joint

cladding line

1'-6" 40'-0"

cladding angle

SECONDARY BEAM cladding

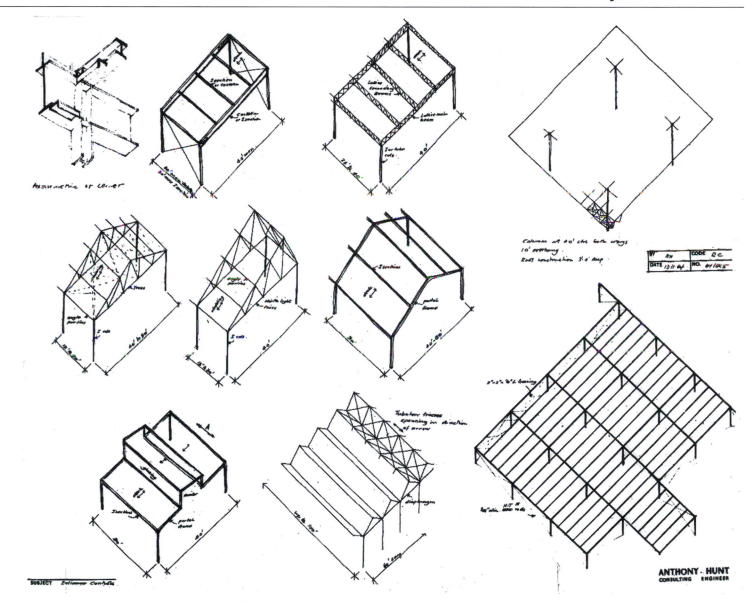

Reliance Controls Factory, Swindon

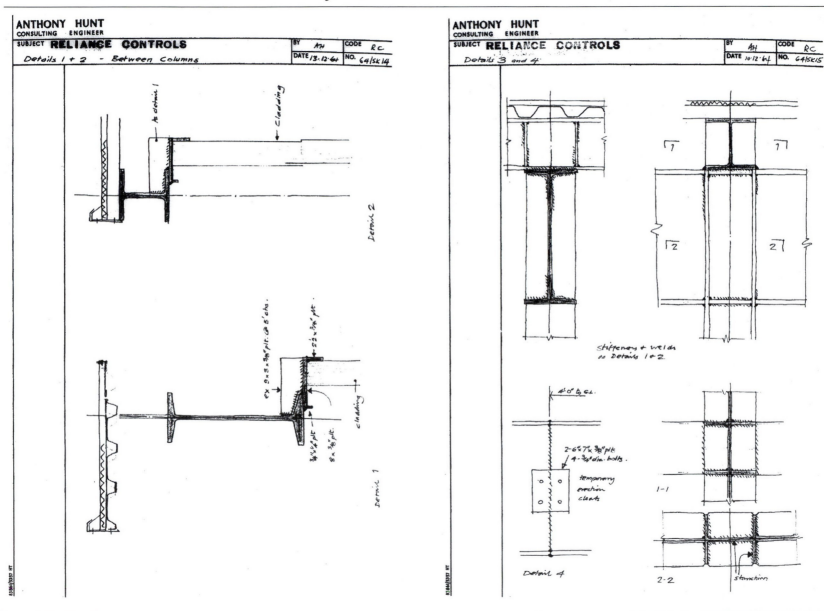

ANTHONY HUNT
CONSULTING ENGINEER
SUBJECT **RELIANCE CONTROLS**
Details 1 + 2 — Between Columns
BY AH CODE RC
DATE 13·12·64 NO. 64/SK14

ANTHONY HUNT
CONSULTING ENGINEER
SUBJECT **RELIANCE CONTROLS**
Details 3 and 4
BY AH CODE RC
DATE 10·12·64 NO. 64/SK15

New Library

Job: New Library, Leicester

Client: University of Leicester

Architect: Castle, Park, Dean, Hook

Date: 1966 – Built 1969 to later design
          using similar principles

- Aim – to design a fully air-
  conditioned building within
  existing UGC limits
- Reinforced concrete high
  mass structure
- Hollow box columns and beams,
  ceiling ducts formed between
  precast Tee floor beams
- No metalwork ducting
- System patented as 'Structair'

New Library, Leicester

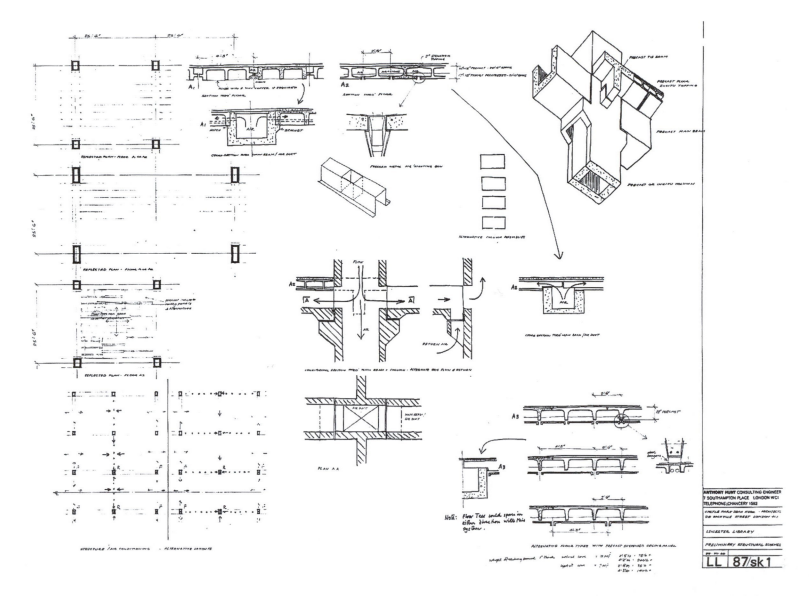

Zip-Up House

Job: Zip-Up House

Client: Ideal Home Exhibition

Architect: Richard and Su Rogers

Date: 1966 – Competition winner not built

- Advanced technology
- Minimum number of components (two)
  Identical floor and roof panel
  Identical wall panels
- Panels are composite aluminium outer
  and inner skins with rigid eurethane
  core
- Variable support conditions according
  to site

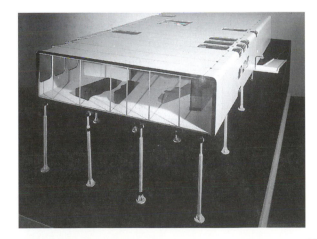

Zip-Up House

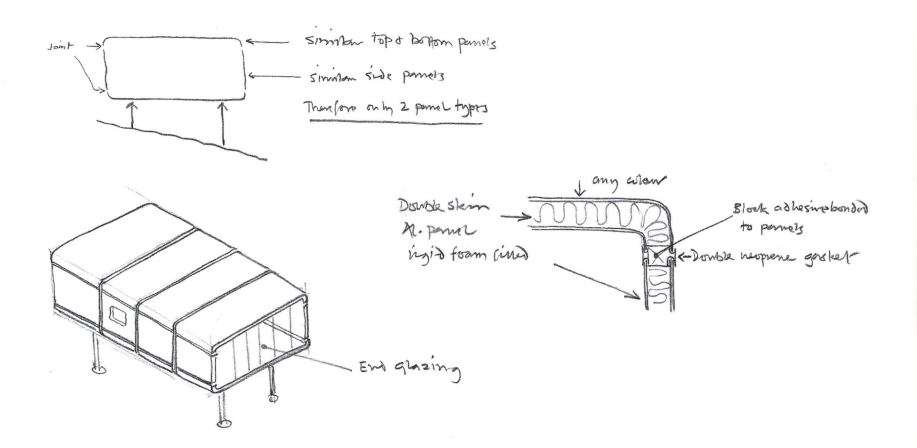

Zip-up House

Joint

Similar top & bottom panels

Similar side panels

Therefore only 2 panel types

Double skin
Al. panel
rigid foam filled

any colour

Block adhesive bonded
to panels

← Double neoprene gasket

End glazing

Sobell Pavilions for Apes and Monkeys

Job: Sobell Pavilions for Apes and
            Monkeys

Client: The Zoological Society of London

Architect: John Toovey, Architect to the Zoo

Date: 1973 – Built

- The brief was to design a range of
  new enclosures for a range of ape
  and monkey species to replace the
  sub-standard existing cages
- Tubular steel space frames were
  developed in different sizes and
  configurations with a mesh cladding
- For the very active chimpanzee
  colony a spring system was
  developed for the vertical mesh
  which acts like a trampoline

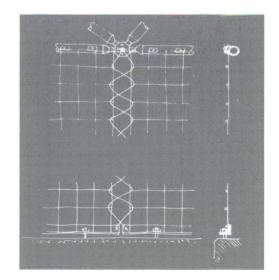

Sobell Pavilions for Apes and Monkeys

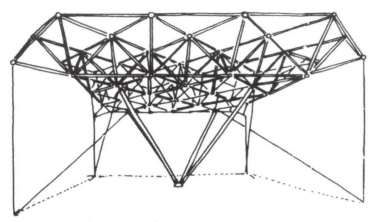

SPACE FRAME - LONDON ZOO
Centrally supported with tension cables for stability

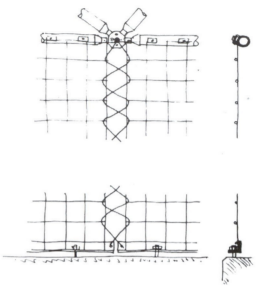

VERTICAL MESH PANEL LINK
(slimmer steel strand)

CABLE + MAST SUPPORTED SPACE FRAME
AS ENTRANCE CANOPY

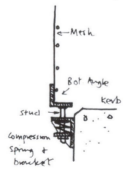

Mesh

Bot Angle

Kerb

stud

Compression
Spring +
bracket

GORILLA MESH DETAIL
FOR "TRAMPOLINE" EFFECT

Sainsbury Centre, UEA

Job: Sainsbury Centre, UEA, Norwich

Client: University of East Anglia and
           Sir Robert Sainsbury

Architect: Foster Associates

Date: 1974–75 – Built

- The first big multi-purpose 'shed'
- Complex brief from two
  combined clients:
  Art gallery, study centre, senior
  common room, restaurant,
  conservation and storage
- Range of structural options
  considered:
    - *Column-free clear span*
    - *Portal frame – steel*
    - *Space frame roof and walls –
      Aluminium Triodetic system*
    - **Prismatic lattice trusses and
      columns in steel*
- Cladding outside or inside
- *Final design with super plastic
  aluminium panels for roof and walls
  linked with neoprene ladder gaskets

Sainsbury Centre, UEA, Norwich

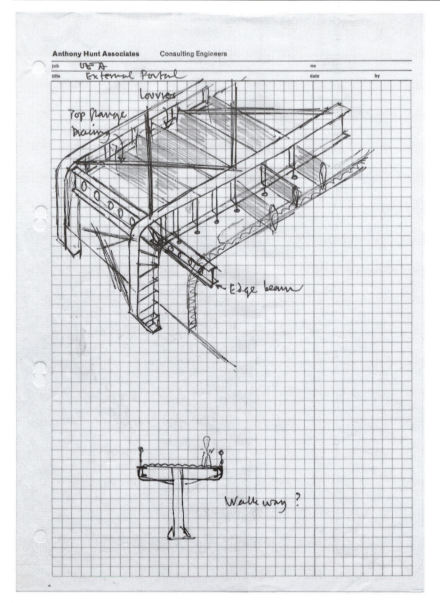

Anthony Hunt Associates   Consulting Engineers

job UEA A
title External Portal

Louvres

Top flange
bracing

Edge beam

Walkway?

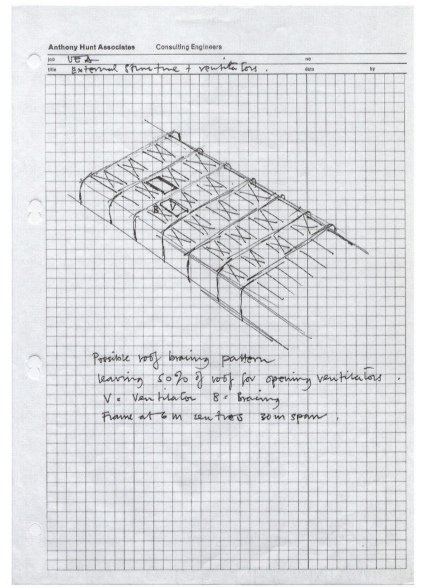

Anthony Hunt Associates   Consulting Engineers

job UEA A
title External structure + ventilators.

Possible roof bracing pattern
leaving 50% of roof for opening ventilators.
V = ventilator B = bracing
Frame at 6 m centres 30 m span.

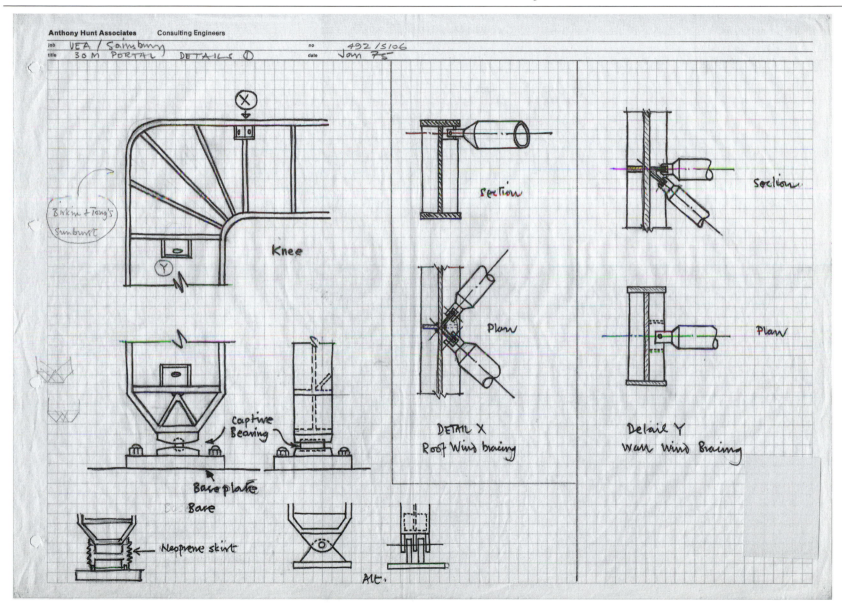

Anthony Hunt Associates   Consulting Engineers

job UEA / Sainsbury   no 492/5106
title 30M PORTAL DETAILS ①   date Jan 75

Barbra + Tony's Sunburst

Knee

Section

Section

Plan

Plan

captive Bearing

Base plate
Das Base

DETAIL X
Roof Wind bracing

Detail Y
Wall Wind Bracing

Neoprene skirt

Alt.

Sainsbury Centre, UEA, Norwich

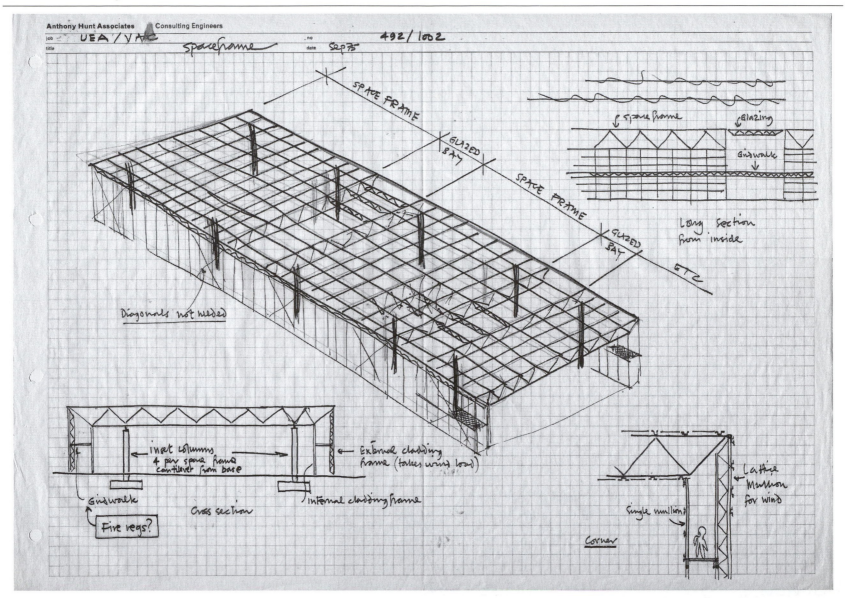

Anthony Hunt Associates — Consulting Engineers

job UEA / VAC   no 492/1002

title spaceframe   date Sep 75

SPACE FRAME

GLAZED BAY

SPACE FRAME

GLAZED BAY

ETC

space frame

glazing

Gridwalk

Long section from inside

Diagonals not needed

inset columns
4 per space frame
cantilever from base

External cladding frame (takes wind load)

Internal cladding frame

Gridwalk

Cross section

Five regs?

single mullion

Lattice mullion for wind

Corner

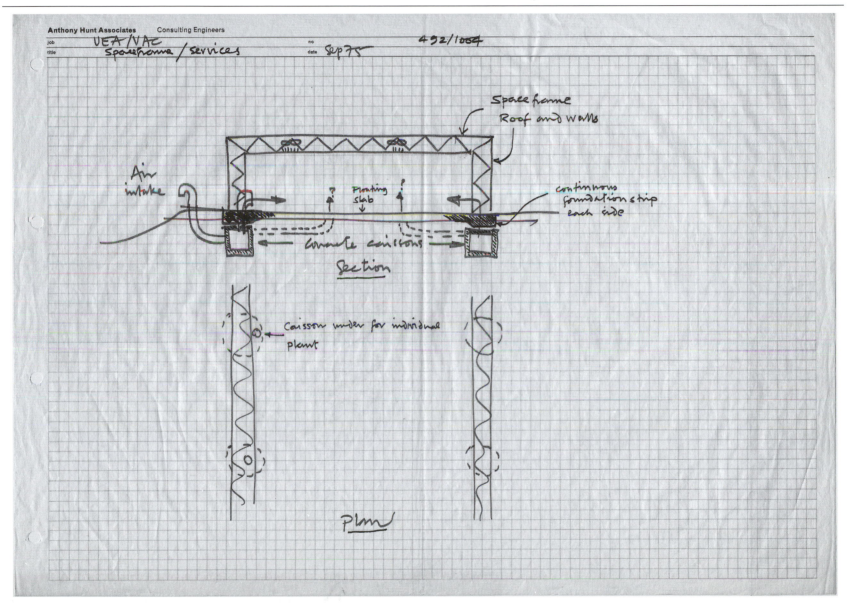

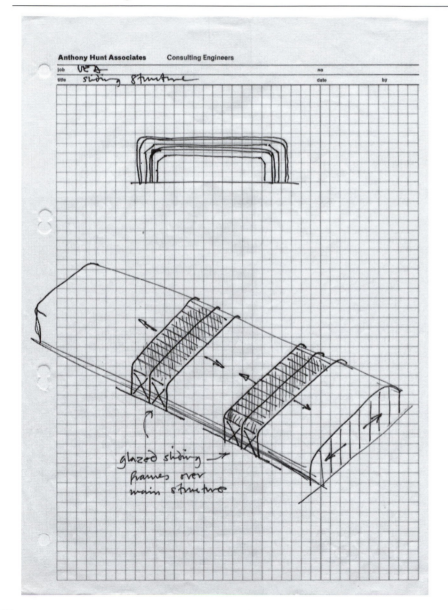

Anthony Hunt Associates Consulting Engineers

job UEA
title sliding structure

glazed sliding
frames over
main structure

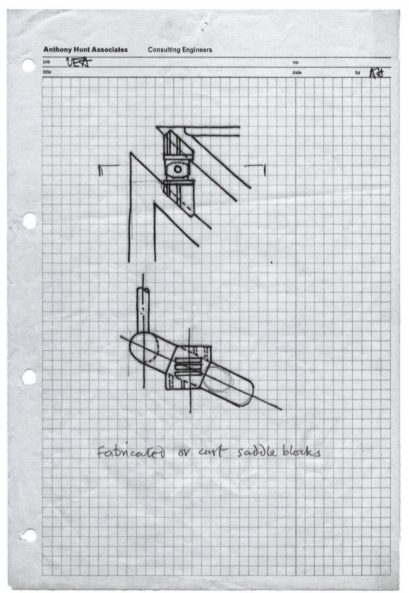

Anthony Hunt Associates Consulting Engineers

job UEA
title   by AH

Fabricated or cast saddle blocks

UEA Ramp Stair ⑦ Apr 77   UEA Ramp Stair ⑧ Apr 77.

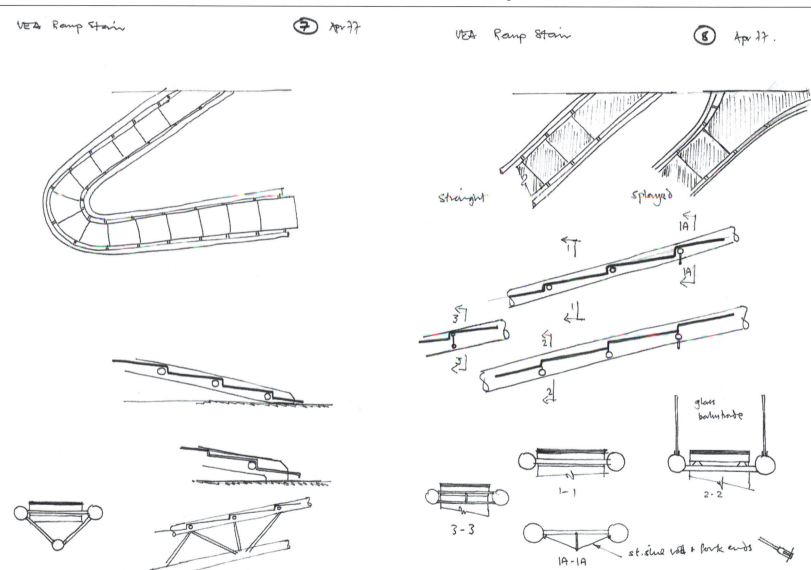

straight   splayed

glass
balustrade

1-1   2-2

3-3

1A-1A   st. steel rod + fork ends

Hopkins House

Job: Hopkins House, London

Client: Mr and Mrs Michael Hopkins

Architect: Mr and Mrs Michael Hopkins

Date: 1976 – Built

- A two-storey steel frame building with profile steel first floor and roof decks
- Aim: to use a minimum number of small scale structural elements in a similar way to the Eames house, California
- Off the shelf lattice beam elements not available so designed in house
- 2 lattice beam types, 1 perimeter beam, 1 column type and 1 X-bracing member
- First floor composite profile steel and plywood deck acting as a stiff diaphragm

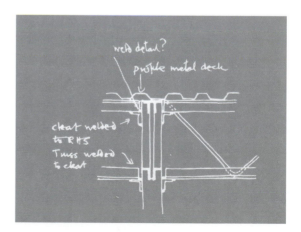

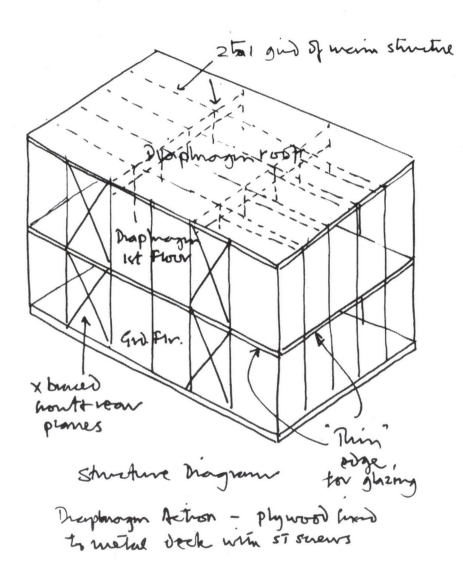

2 steel grid of main structure

Diaphragm roof

Diaphragm 1st Floor

Grd. Flr.

x braced front & rear planes

"Thin" edge, for glazing

Structure Diagram

Diaphragm Action — plywood fixed to metal deck with ST screws

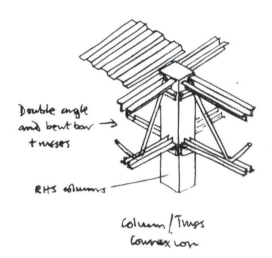

Double angle and bent bar trusses

RHS columns

Column / Truss Connexion

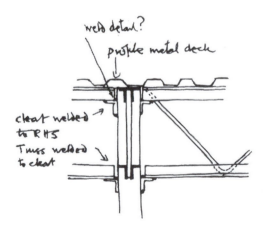

weld detail?

profile metal deck

cleat welded to RHS

Truss welded to cleat

Alexandra Road Housing Development

Job: Alexandra Road Housing
Development, London

Client: London Borough of Camden

Architect: Neave Brown/Camden Borough
Council

Date: 1978 – Built

- Major London housing development
- All in-situ concrete construction –
  walls and floors
- Anti-vibration bearings beneath
  walls to counteract the effect from
  adjacent railway

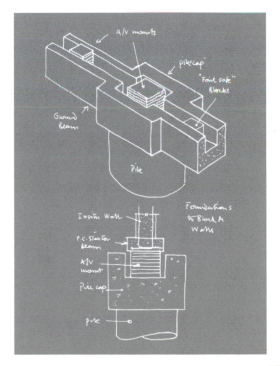

Alexandra Road Housing Development, London

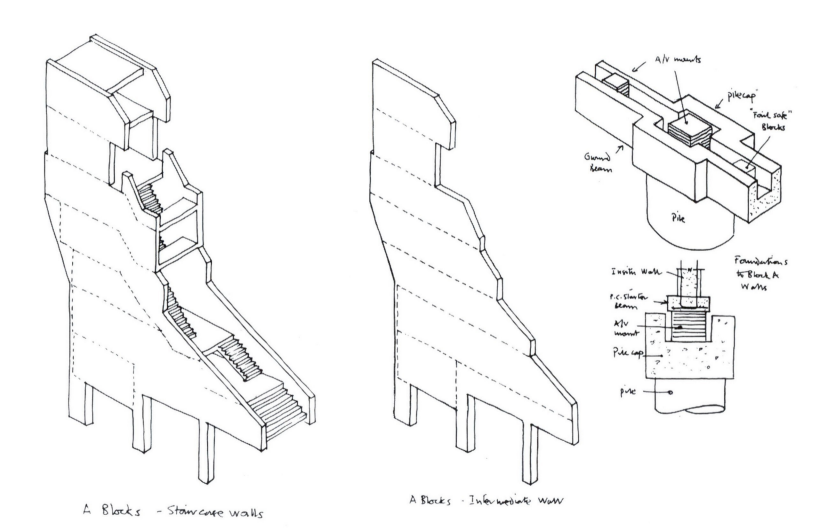

A/V mounts

pilecap

"Fail safe" Blocks

Ground Beam

Pile

Insitu Wall

Foundations to Block A Walls

P.C. Starter Beam

A/V mount

Pile cap

pile

A Blocks - Staircase walls

A Blocks - Intermediate Wall

NAPP Pharmaceutical HQ

Cambridge

Job: NAPP Pharmaceutical HQ,
            Cambridge

Client: North American Pharmaceutical
            Products

Architect: Richard Rogers Partnership

Date: 1978 – Competition winner, unbuilt

- Exploring the idea of large span
  uninterrupted space via a masted
  structure with tension hangers
- All functions operate within the
  overall envelope
- Alternative structural solutions
  explored
- Different stability systems
  considered

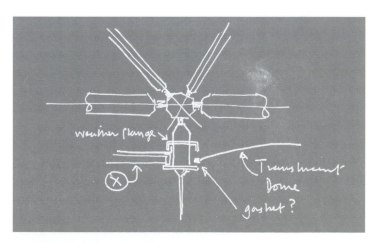

NAPP Pharmaceutical HQ, Cambridge

Brief : 1. 60 m clear span enclosure

2. 8 M clear internal height
with facilities for mezzanines

3. structure to be extendible in
length at each end

4. Services required outside
main enclosure
(what about maintenance
and replacement).

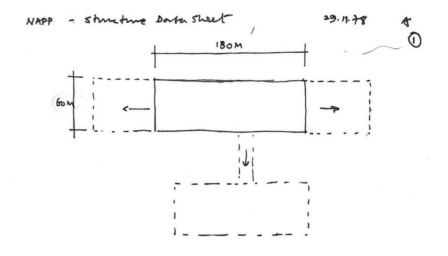

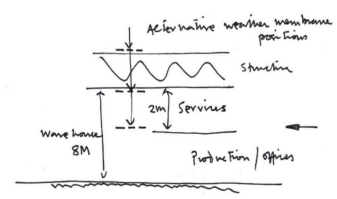

Alternative weather membrane
positions

Structure

2m │ Services

Ware house
8M

Production / offices

if w. membrane was here,
could services be housed
in the open-air ?

Zoning (vertical)

NAPP   original proposal

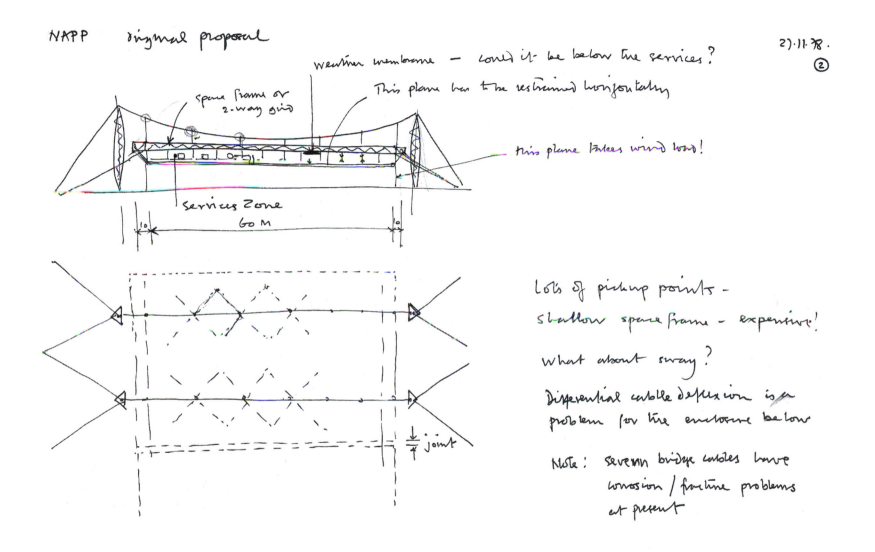

weather membrane — could it be below the services?

This plane has to be restrained horizontally

2).11.78.

②

space frame or
2-way grid

this plane takes wind load!

Services Zone
60 M

Lots of pickup points —
shallow space frame — expensive!

what about sway?

Differential cable deflexion is a
problem for the enclosure below

Note: severn bridge cables have
corrosion / fracture problems
at present

¼ joint

NAPP Pharmaceutical HQ, Cambridge

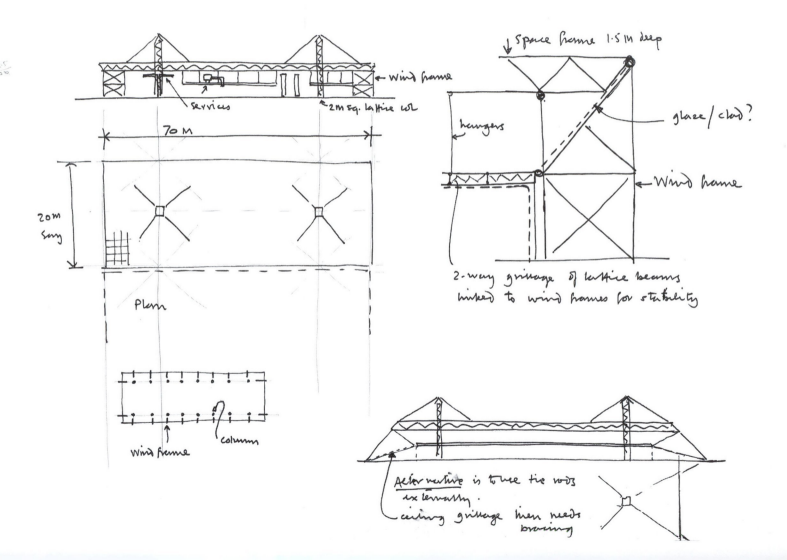

wind frame

services

2M sq. lattice col

70 M

20m long

Plan

wind frame

column

Space frame 1·5 M deep

glaze / clad?

hangers

Wind frame

2-way grillage of lattice beams
linked to wind frames for stability

Alternative is tree tie rods
externally.
ceiling grillage then needs
bracing

NAPP   Structure   1 A   29.11.78   A4

④

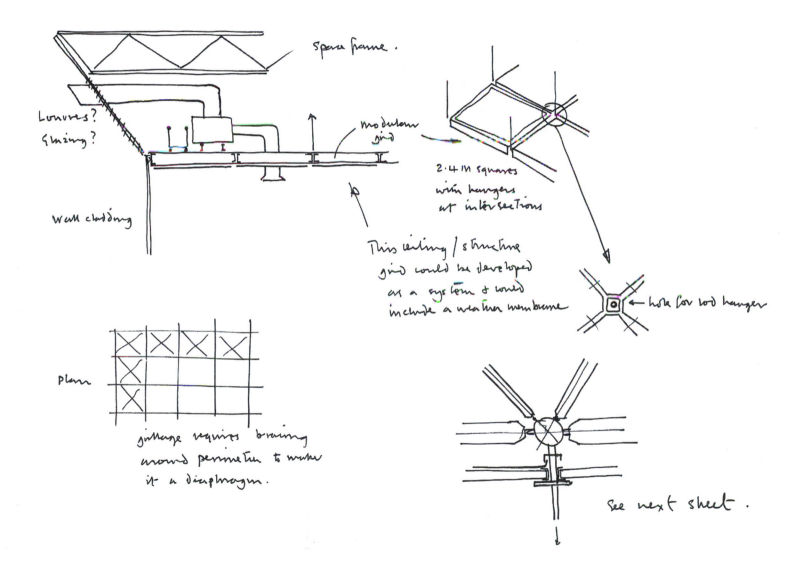

Space frame.

Louvres?
Glazing?

modular
grid

Wall cladding

2.4 M squares
with hangers
at intersections

This ceiling / structure
grid could be developed
as a system & could
include a weather membrane

← hole for rod hanger

plane

jointage requires bracing
around perimeter to make
it a diaphragm.

See next sheet.

NAPP Pharmaceutical HQ, Cambridge

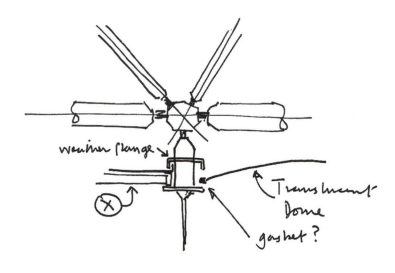

weather flange

"Translucent
Dome

gasket ?

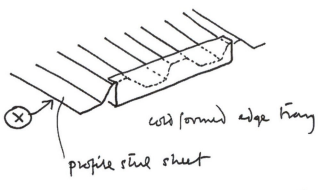

cold formed edge tray

profile steel sheet

"Roof" panel to fit space frame
node module

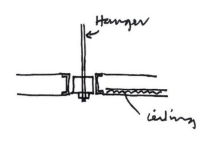

Hanger

ceiling

NAPP   Structure #7   30.11.78   AT

⑨

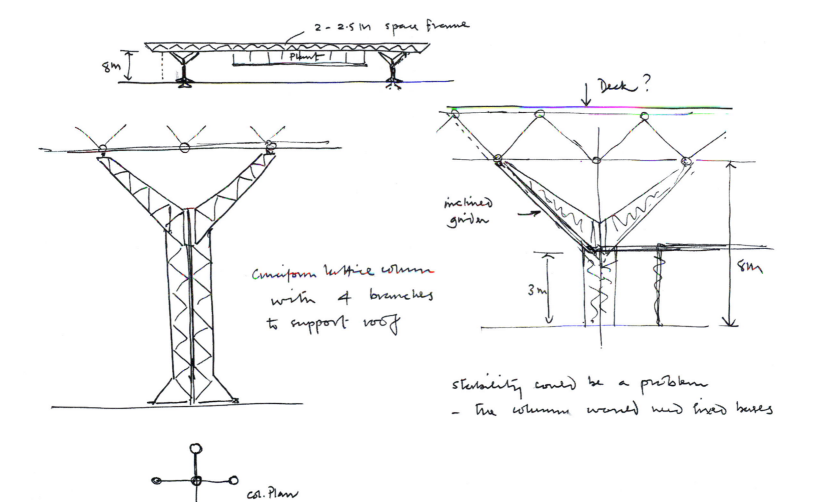

2 - 2.5 m space frame

Plant

8m

Deck ?

Cruciform lattice column
with 4 branches
to support roof

inclined
girder

8m

3 m

col. Plan

stability could be a problem
- the column would need fixed bases

NAPP Pharmaceutical HQ, Cambridge

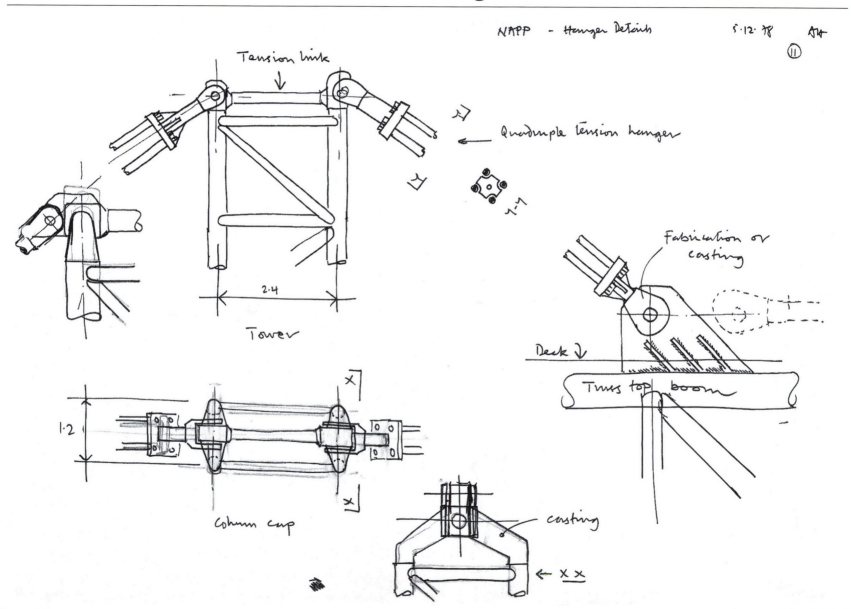

NAPP — Hanger Details   5·12·78   AH

(11)

Tension link

Quadruple tension hanger

Tower

2·4

Fabrication or casting

Deck ↓

Truss top boom

1·2

Column cap

casting

← X X

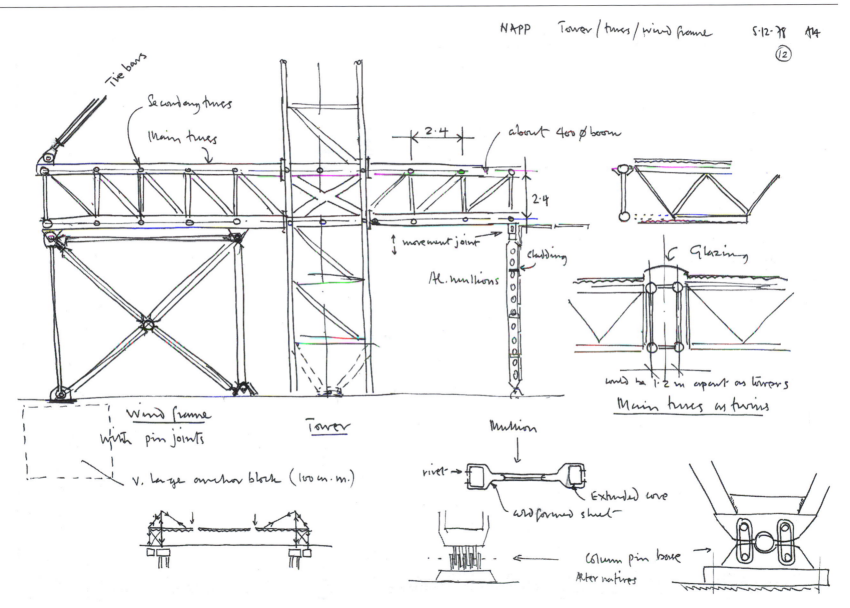

NAPP   Tower / trues / wind frame   5·12·78 A4
⑫

Tie bars

Secondary trues

Main trues

2·4

about 400 ø boom

2·4

movement joint

Al. mullions

cladding

Glazing

would be 1·2 m apart as towers

Main trues as twins

Wind frame
with pin joints

Tower

Mullion

V. large anchor block (100 m.m.)

rivet

Extruded core

cold formed sheel

Column pin base
Alternatives

37

Foster House

Job: Foster House, London

Client: Norman and Wendy Foster

Architects: Norman and Wendy Foster

Date: 1979 – Project

- The proposal was to design a modular building as a private house
- Many options were explored, first using steel components
- A kit of aluminium structural components was developed and prototyped full size

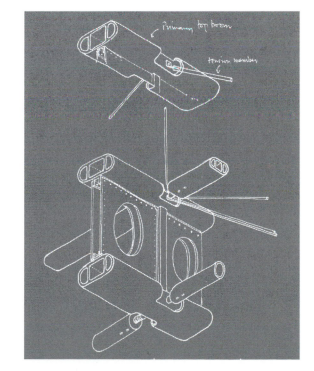

Foster House, London

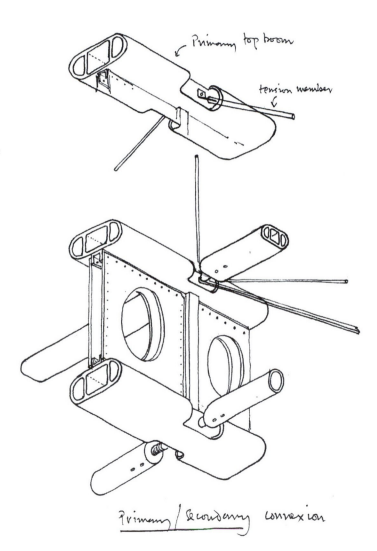

Primary top boom

tension member

Primary / Secondary connexion

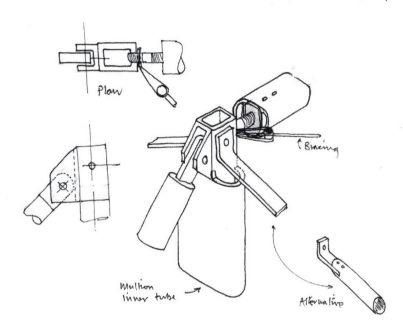

Plan

Bracing

Mullion
inner tube

Alternative

Top of wind mullion

Alternative

Bottom boom +
diagonal for
secondaries

Mullion - main tube / bracing alternatives

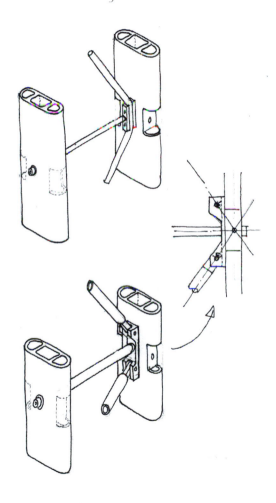

Top boom

Strut-

bottom boom

tie

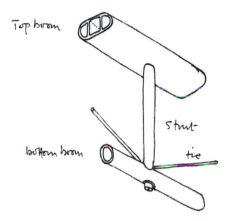

Secondary beams - centre connexion

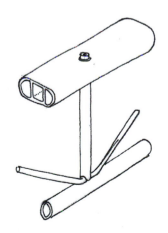

Inmos Microelectronics

Job: Inmos Microelectronics, Waferfab
           Plant, Newport

Client: Inmos (UK)

Architect: Richard Rogers Partnership

Date: 1980 – Built

- The NAPP project developed with a more complex brief
- Client requirements:
  Column free spaces
  External access to all major services plant for change and maintenance
- 24 hour/365 days/year operation
- Minimum services within floor
- Capable of future extension without disruption to production
- Very short design and building programme
- Use of minimum number of large structural steel elements with stainless steel single pin connections throughout
- Early use of computer analysis for structural design

Inmos Microelectronics, Waferfab Plant, Newport

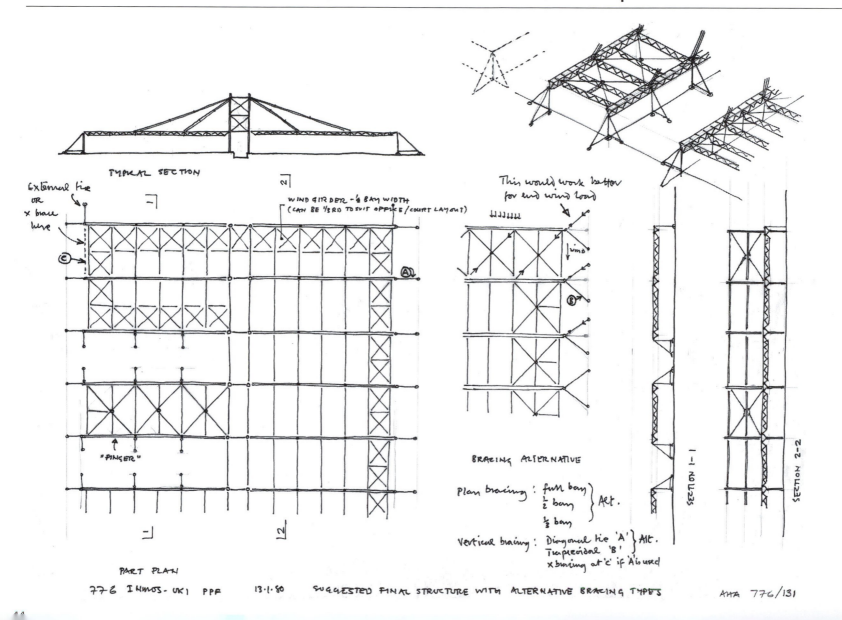

TYPICAL SECTION

External tie
or
X brace
here

WIND GIRDER - ½ BAY WIDTH
(CAN BE ⅓ RD TO SUIT OFFICE/COURT LAYOUT)

This would work better
for end wind load

wind

"PINGER"

BRACING ALTERNATIVE

Plan bracing : full bay⎫
½ bay⎬ Alt.
⅓ bay⎭

Vertical bracing : Diagonal tie 'A' ⎫ Alt.
Trapezoidal 'B' ⎭
X bracing at 'c' if 'A' is used

SECTION 1-1

SECTION 2-2

PART PLAN

776 INMOS-UK1 PPF   13·1·80   SUGGESTED FINAL STRUCTURE WITH ALTERNATIVE BRACING TYPES   AHA 776/131

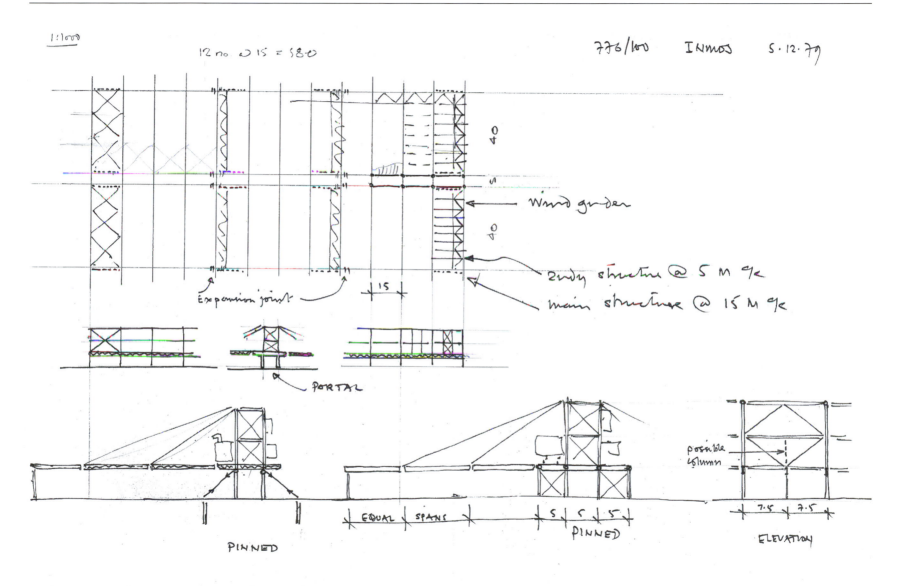

1:1000

12 no. @ 15 = 180

776/100   INMOS   5.12.79

Wind girder

2ndy structure @ 5 M %

main structure @ 15 M %

Expansion joint

15

PORTAL

PINNED

EQUAL SPANS

5 | 5 | 5
PINNED

possible column

7.5 | 7.5

ELEVATION

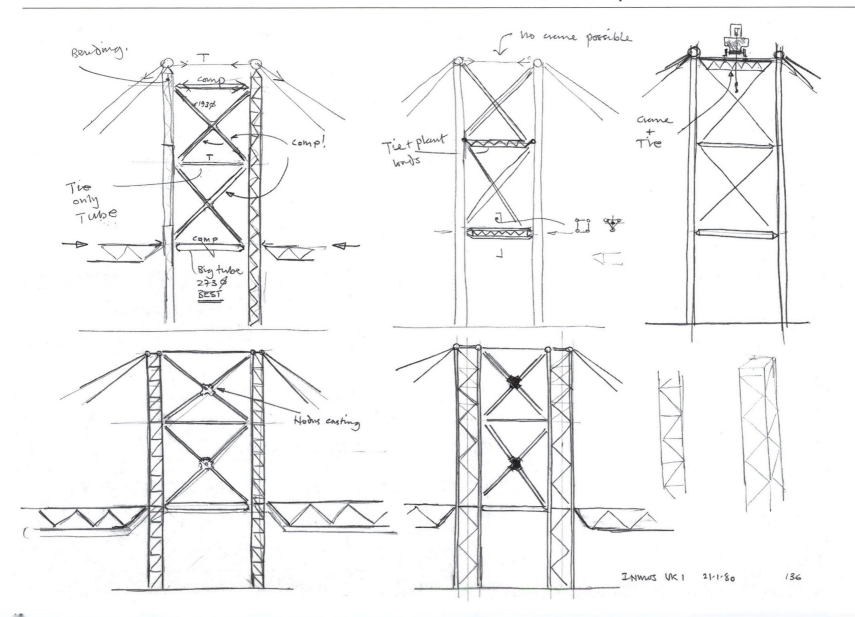

INMOS UK1   21·1·'80   136

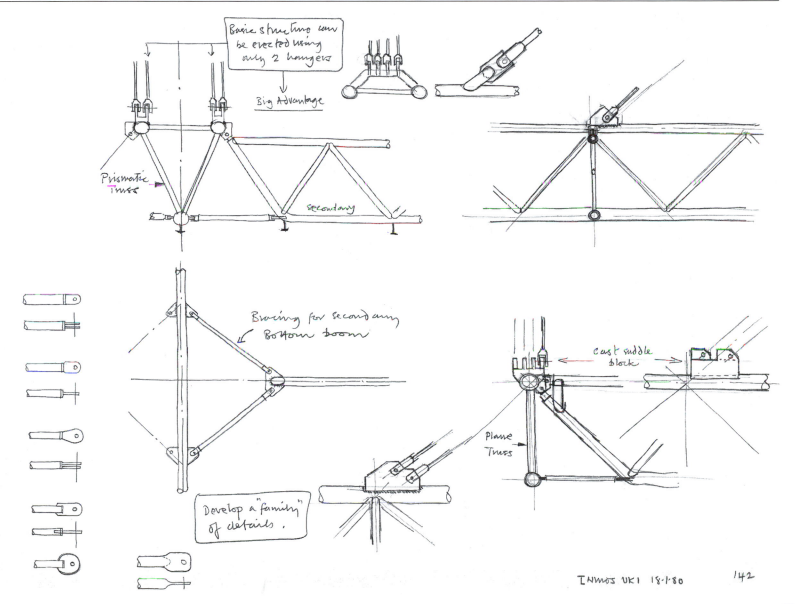

Basic structure can be erected using only 2 hangers

Big Advantage

Prismatic Truss

secondary

Bracing for secondary Bottom boom

Develop a "family" of details.

cast saddle block

Plane Truss

INMOS UKI 18·1·80   142

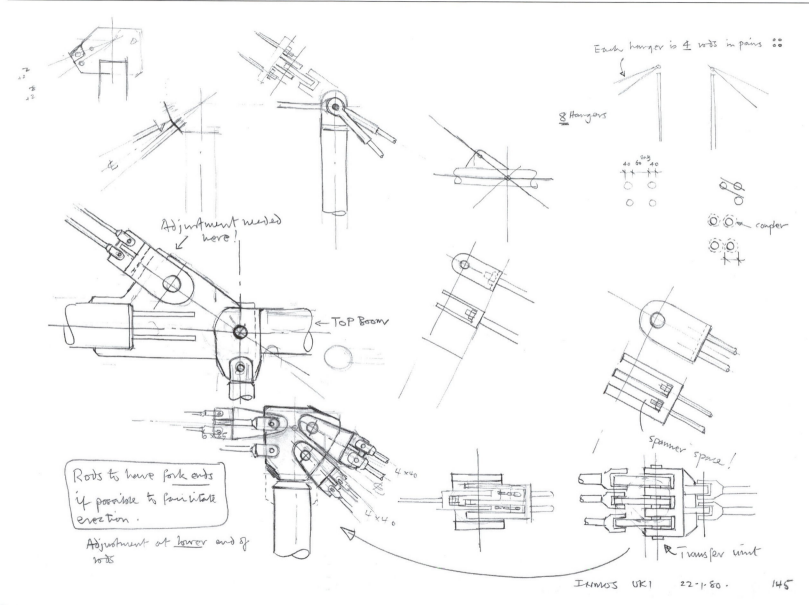

Each hanger is 4 rods in pairs

8 Hangers

Adjustment needed here!

← TOP BOOM

coupler

Rods to have fork ends if possible to facilitate erection.

Adjustment at lower end of rods

4 x 40

4 x 4 0

spanner space!

← Transfer unit

INMOS UK1   22-1-80.   145

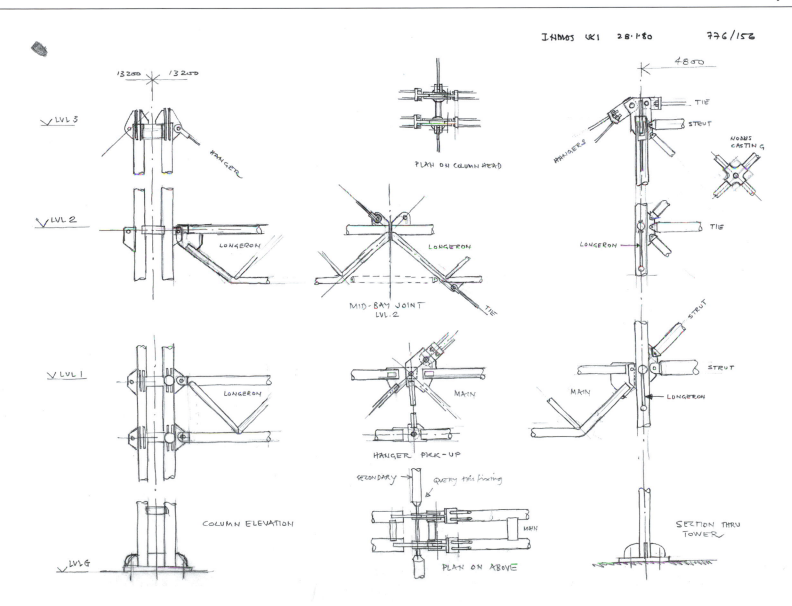

INMOS UK1   28.1.80   776/156

LVL 3

LVL 2

LVL 1

LVL G

13200   13200

HANGER

LONGERON

LONGERON

COLUMN ELEVATION

PLAN ON COLUMN HEAD

LONGERON

MID-BAY JOINT
LVL. 2

TIE

MAIN

HANGER PICK-UP

SECONDARY   QUERY this fixing

MAIN

PLAN ON ABOVE

4850

TIE

STRUT

HANGERS

NODES
CASTING

TIE

LONGERON

STRUT

STRUT

MAIN

LONGERON

SECTION THRU
TOWER

Amphitheatre

Job: Amphitheatre, London Zoo

Client: The Zoological Society of London

Architect: John Toovey

Date: 1983 – Built

- Simple tensile membrane structure on a confined site
- One of the classic cone designs with perimeter struts and tie-downs

Amphitheatre, London Zoo

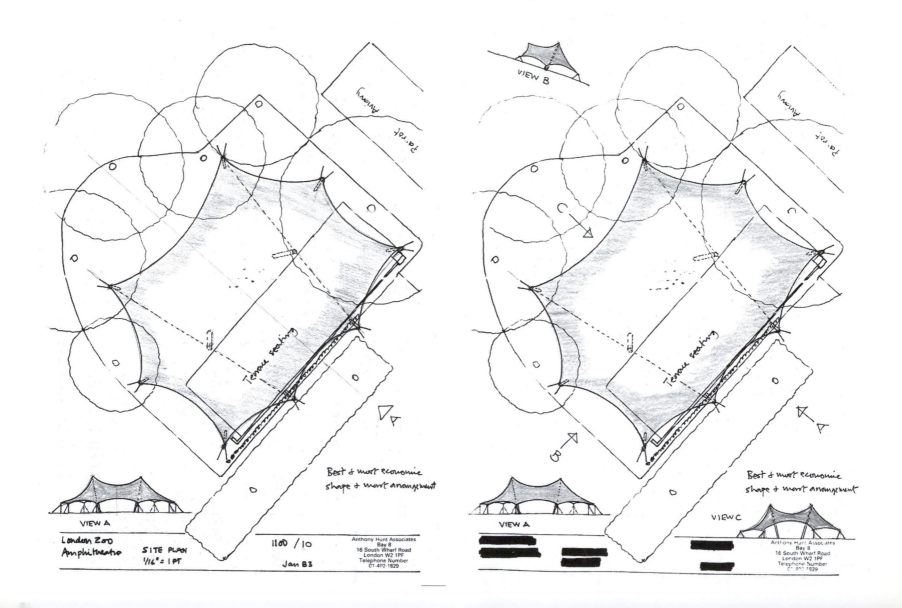

VIEW B

VIEW A

Terrace seating

Best & most economic
shape & most arrangement

London Zoo
Amphitheatre

SITE PLAN
1/16" = 1FT

1100 / 10

Jan 83

Anthony Hunt Associates
Bay 8
16 South Wharf Road
London W2 1PF
Telephone Number
01-402-1829

VIEW A

VIEW C

Terrace seating

Best & most economic
shape & most arrangement

Anthony Hunt Associates
Bay 8
16 South Wharf Road
London W2 1PF
Telephone Number
01-402-1829

Access Tower for Greyfriars Redevelopment

Job: Access Tower for Greyfriars
 Redevelopment, Ipswich

Client: Willis Faber Dumas

Architect: Michael Hopkins and Partners

Date: 1984 – Built

- Conversion of a car park structure
  with offices
- New access and fire escape
  external structure
- Simple braced steel frame tower
- Teflon-glass cone membrane
  cladding units all similar and with a
  boundary steel frame producing
  discrete bolt-on elements

Access Tower for Greyfriars Redevelopment, Ipswich

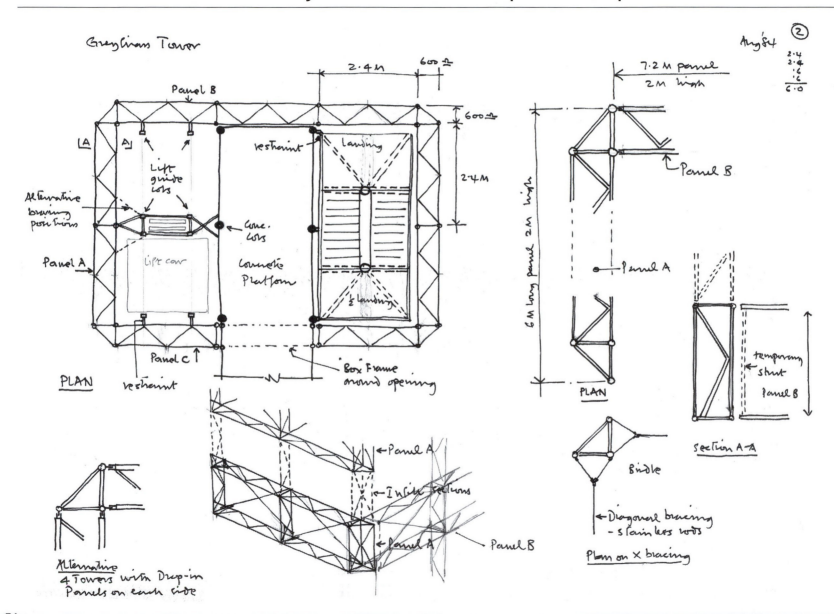

Greyfriars Tower

Aug '84 ②

2·4
2·4
·6
·6
6·0

Panel B

2·4 M   600 ⌀

600 ⌀

2·4 M

restraint

landing

Lift
guide
rods

⌊A   A⌋

Alternative
bracing
positions

Conc.
rods

Panel A

Lift car

Concrete
Platform

⅓ landing

Box Frame
around opening

PLAN

restraint

Panel C ↑

restraint

7·2 M panel
2M high

← Panel B

6 M long panel 2M high

•─ Panel A

PLAN

temporary
strut
Panel B

Section A-A

Bridle

← Panel A

↔ Infill sections

← Panel A

Panel B

← Diagonal bracing
– stainless rods

Plan on X bracing

Alternative
4 Towers with Drop-in
Panels on each side

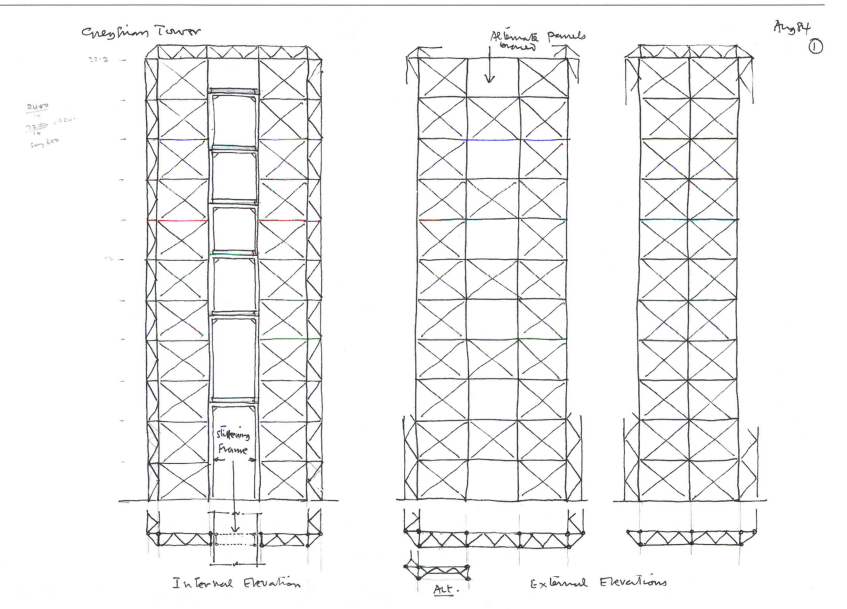

Greyfriars Tower

Alternate Panels (braced)

Aug 84

①

Internal Elevation

Alt.

External Elevations

stiffening Frame

Don Valley Athletics Stadium

Sheffield

Job: Don Valley Athletics Stadium, Sheffield

Client: City of Sheffield

Architect: Sheffield Design and Building Services

Date: 1987 – Built

- Brief – to produce a landmark for Sheffield as part of the Don Valley regeneration
- Design developed via design workshops with all consultants in a conference centre
- Membrane roof options proposed in initial discussion, accepted and developed
- Tension assisted cantilever roof form proposed to give best sight lines
- Pin-jointed steel frame plus precast concrete seating for simplicity and speed
- Raft foundation to cope with underground mine working
- Teflon-glass rather than PVC-polyester for long life and elegance

Don Valley Athletics Stadium, Sheffield

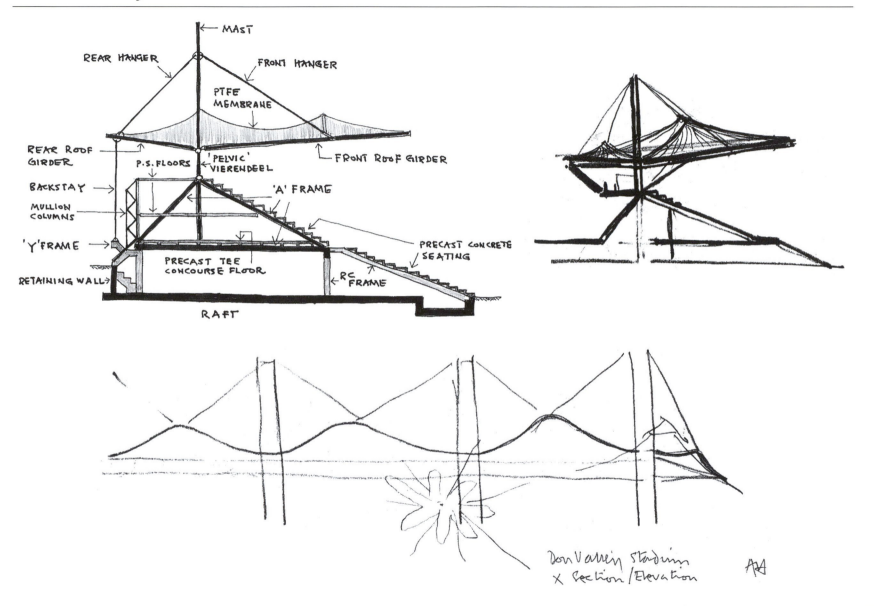

MAST

REAR HANGER

FRONT HANGER

PTFE MEMBRANE

REAR ROOF GIRDER

P.S. FLOORS

'PELVIC' VIERENDEEL

FRONT ROOF GIRDER

BACKSTAY

'A' FRAME

MULLION COLUMNS

'Y' FRAME

PRECAST CONCRETE SEATING

PRECAST TEE CONCOURSE FLOOR

RC FRAME

RETAINING WALL

RAFT

Don Valley Stadium
X Section / Elevation

Waterloo International Terminal

London – First Scheme

Job: Waterloo International Terminal,
            London – First Scheme

Client: British Rail

Architect: British Rail Architects

Date: 1988 – Unbuilt early scheme

- Brief from British Rail Architects to produce a simple repetitive economic clear span solution in pure engineering terms
- Steel prismatic girders and columns
- Cladding a combination of glass over trusses and Teflon-glass membrane between
- Membrane shape achieved via curved trusses and cable tie-downs
- Ideas used as basis of development of final scheme

Waterloo Terminal
1st Scheme for BR Architects

- Clear Span structure – max span about 48 m
                         min span "   35 m
- Plan a mixture of straight & varying curves
- Just a 'train shed' to cover the platforms
- Repetitive main structure at regular spacing
- Translucent
- Fixed platform over existing track layout.
- Lightweight steel structure
- Try combination of glazing & fabric membrane

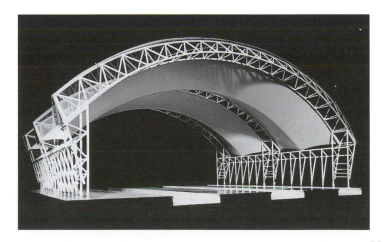

Waterloo International Terminal, London – First Scheme

Waterloo Terminal

1st Scheme

for BR

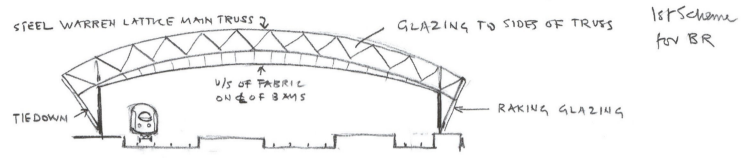

STEEL WARREN LATTICE MAIN TRUSS

GLAZING TO SIDES OF TRUSS

U/S OF FABRIC
ON ℄ OF BAYS

TIE DOWN

RAKING GLAZING

TEFLON GLASS MEMBRANE

GLAZING

CABLE

MAIN TRUSS
+
COLUMN

TIE DOWN CABLES
TO GIVE DOUBLE
CURVATURE TO
MEMBRANE

EDGE GLAZING

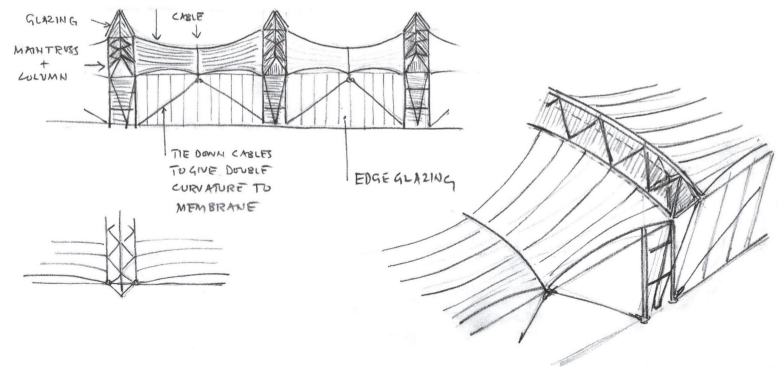

Terminal 5 Heathrow

London

Job: Terminal 5 Heathrow, London

Client: BAA plc

Architect: YRM Architects

Date: 1989 – Competition entry

- Aim – to produce very large, dramatic clear span spaces
- An exercise in structural ideas on a very large scale
- Main Terminal:
  - Large concrete columns for stability
  - Steel prismatic primary trusses fabric clad to provide overhead services routes for air supply
  - two-way secondary lattice of slender pre-stressed steel girders supporting a fully glazed roof with varying transparency/translucence
  - Reinforced concrete structure for floors
- Satellite:
  - Scaled down version of main terminal

Terminal 5 Heathrow, London

ROOF STRUCTURE ALTERNATIVES

CLEAR SPAN :

CABLE NET WITH MASTS

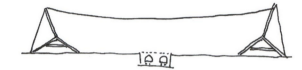

CABLE / MAST WITH BOW STRING TRUSSES

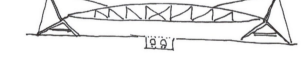

MULTI CABLE / MAST WITH LATTICE ARCH

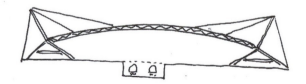

NONE OF THESE ALLOW FOR PHASED CONSTRUCTION?

AH TS ②
    05/80

ROOF STRUCTURE ALTERNATIVES

DOUBLE SPAN:

CABLE NET

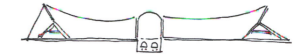

BOWSTRING GIRDERS

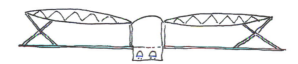

LAMELLA ARCHES

PHASED CONSTRUCTION POSSIBLE BUT DIFFICULT

ROOF STRUCTURE ALTERNATIVES

MULTI SPAN (CHANGED DIRECTION OF PRIMARIES)

3 EQUAL SPANS

BOWSTRING

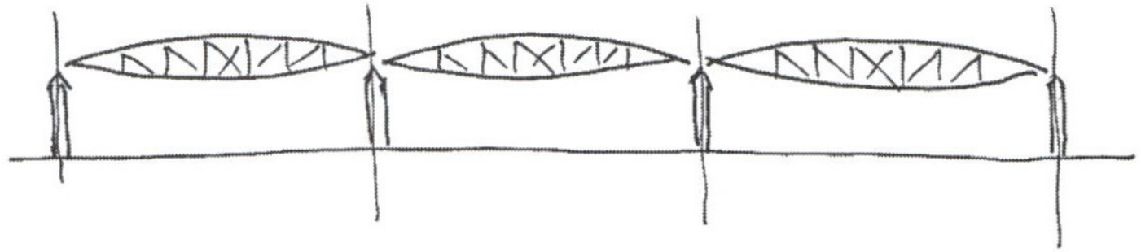

VAULT

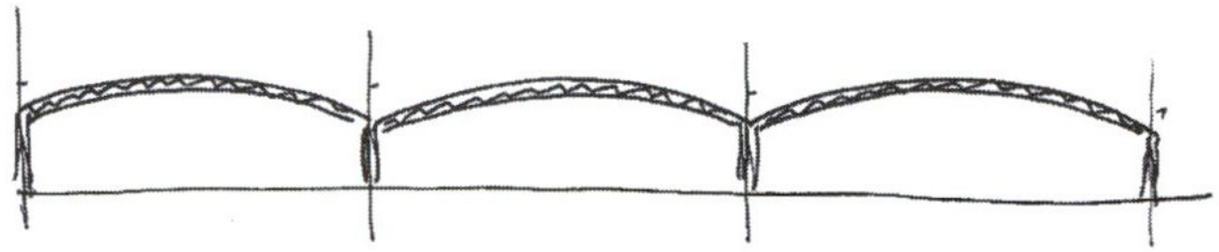

VAULT TO GROUND
   — very efficient structure

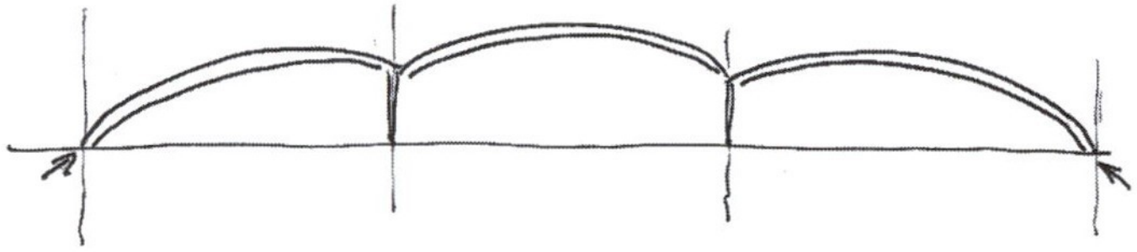

SECONDARIES

ORTHOGONAL OR DIAGONAL DISPOSITION

HORIZONTAL OR CURVED ?

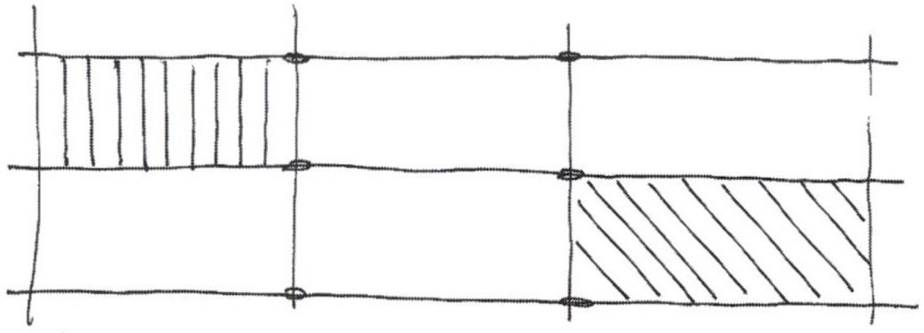

AH TS ③
01/5/89

④

AH T5
05/89

ROOF STRUCTURE ALTERNATIVES

DEVELOP THE EFFICIENT ARCH FORM TO PRODUCE
A SOARING SPACE WITH MINIMUM STRUCTURE

VAULT IN BOTH DIRECTIONS TO MAKE THE STRUCTURE
EVEN MORE EFFICIENT

USE THE MAIN ARCHES FOR AIR DISTRIBUTION -
DUAL PURPOSE

INCORPORATE TENSION ELEMENTS INTO THE SECONDARY STRUCTURE

USE ONLY TRIED & TESTED MATERIALS & KNOWN TECHNOLOGY
- STEEL FOR SPEED, ACCURACY & COST

THE STRUCTURE SHOULD BE PRECISE & ELEGANT, REFLECTING
THE SPIRIT OF FLIGHT.

MINIMUM WEIGHT STRUCTURE FOR MAXIMUM EFFECT

STRUCTURE IS A REFLECTION OF NATURAL FORMS

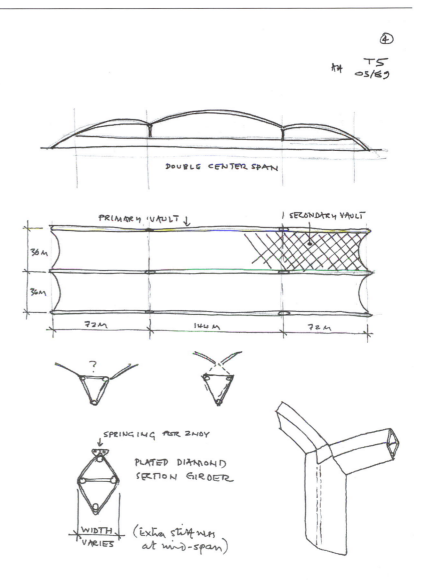

DOUBLE CENTER SPAN

PRIMARY VAULT ↓   SECONDARY VAULT

36 M

36 M

72 M   144 M   72 M

?

SPRINGING FOR 2NDY ↓

PLATED DIAMOND
SECTION GIRDER

WIDTH
VARIES   (extra strands
at mid-span)

Terminal 5 Heathrow, London

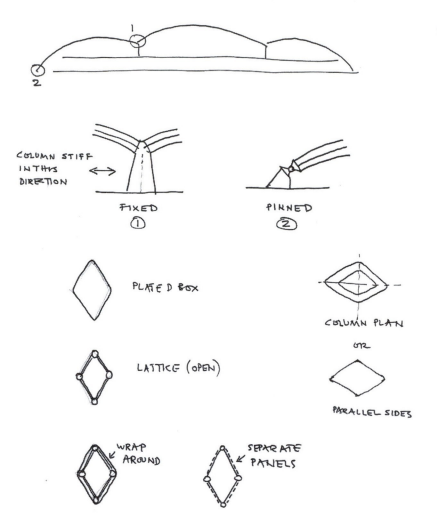

MAIN ARCHES / COLUMNS

FIXED JOINT BETWEEN ARCH & COLUMN REDUCES ARCH
BENDING & DEFLEXION UNDER OUT OF BALANCE LOADING

OUTBOARD JOINT SHOULD BE PINNED

ARCHES CAN BE BOX GIRDERS — PLATED

OPEN LATTICE — EFFICIENT BUT VISUALLY RESTLESS

CLAD LATTICES — LIGHT, CLEAN SURFACES
DUAL PURPOSE (AIR)

CLADDING MUST BE INCOMBUSTIBLE — TEFLON/GLASS
FABRIC

AM. T5 ⑥
05/89

ROOF SECONDARY STRUCTURE

MOST EFFICIENT IS A VAULT AGAIN.

ARCH

TIED ARCH

STRESSED TIED ARCH

- PRESTRESSED AGAINST WIND UPLIFT OR CURVED TIE TO AVOID COMPRESSIONS

  BALANCED FORCE SYSTEM EVEN AT END CONDITION IF ON DIAGONAL

  CROSS ARCHES FOR STABILITY — PRODUCES DIAGRID

  CROSS TIES IN LOWER PLANE TO COMPLETE DIAGRID

  + IMPROVE RESTRAINT TO PRIMARIES

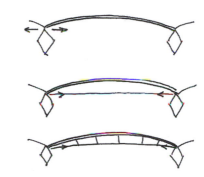

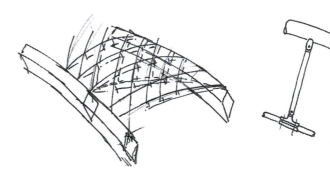

WIND → PRESSURE ↑ SUCTION

PIN

SLIDING JOINT

AM . TS 05/89 ⑦

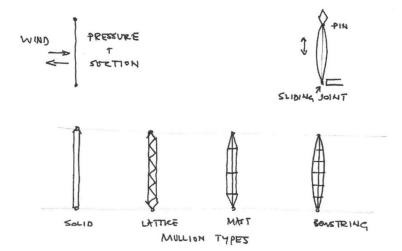

SOLID   LATTICE   MAST   BOWSTRING

MULLION TYPES

GLAZING MULLIONS

WALL STRUCTURE HAS TO RESIST WIND IN TWO DIRECTIONS
THEREFORE MULLION SHOULD BE SYMMETRICAL

NEEDS MAXIMUM GIRTH AT POINT OF MAX BENDING (MID HEIGHT)

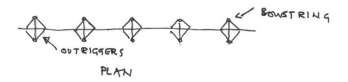

BOWSTRING

OUTRIGGERS

PLAN

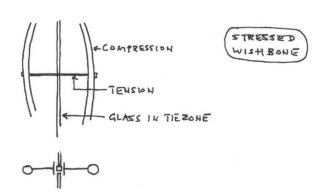

← COMPRESSION

TENSION

GLASS IN TIE ZONE

STRESSED WISHBONE

AH TS ⑧
05/89

"BASE" SUPERSTRUCTURE

CRITERIA : SPEED, REPETITION, FUTURE CHANGE, COST

STEEL FRAME WITH TARTAN GRID FOR VERTICAL MOVEMENT
(STAIRS, TRAVELATORS, LIFTS, SERVICES).

POURED CONCRETE ON METAL DECK - COMPOSITE
ACTION, 2-WAY SPANNING, FULL CONTINUITY
GRID TO SUIT PLANNING - 10·8 M SUGGESTED

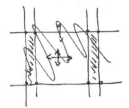 

I BEAMS   UC COLUMNS   "HOLORIB" DECK + RC SLAB

SUBSTRUCTURE

MAIN ROOF COLUMNS   - SINGLE UNDERREAMED PILES

"BASE" SUPERSTRUCTURE   - SINGLE STRAIGHT SHAFT PILE
BENEATH EACH COLUMN

BASEMENT   - WATERTIGHT RC CONSTRUCTION

PERIMETER WALL   - DIAPHRAGM OR CONTIGUOUS PILES

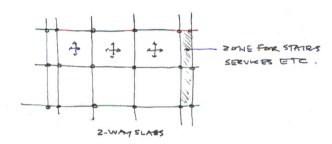

ZONE FOR STAIRS
SERVICES ETC.

2-WAY SLABS

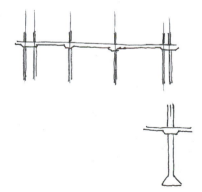

A4   T5
05/89

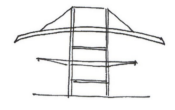

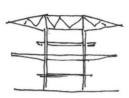

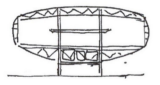

SEMI - MONOCOQUE

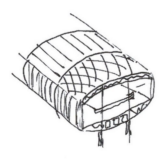

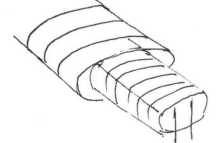

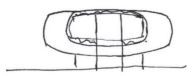

BUILDING GETS WIDER AT CENTRE

SATTELITE BUILDING

STRUCTURE ALTERNATIVES

CENTRAL SPINE STRUCTURE GIVING OVERHANGS FOR VEHICLES

CONSTRAINTS ARE DIFFERENT BUT TRY TO FOLLOW THE

FLAVOUR OF THE TERMINAL

MAINTAIN : SIMPLE REPETITIVE STRUCTURE

USE STEEL FRAME FOR COST & SPEED

(CONSIDER ALUMINIUM FOR ROOF)

CONCRETE FLOORS ON HOLORIB AS COMPOSITE

SATTELITE BUILDING

STRUCTURE ALTERNATIVES

OVERALL ROOF ENVELOPE WITH "BUILDING" UNDERNEATH
COLUMNS SET INBOARD TO SUIT TRAFFIC & BENEFIT STRUCTURE
FABRIC COVERED ROOF ?   — HO.
METAL SKIN ROOF + METAL CEILING - <u>MONOCOQUE</u> !

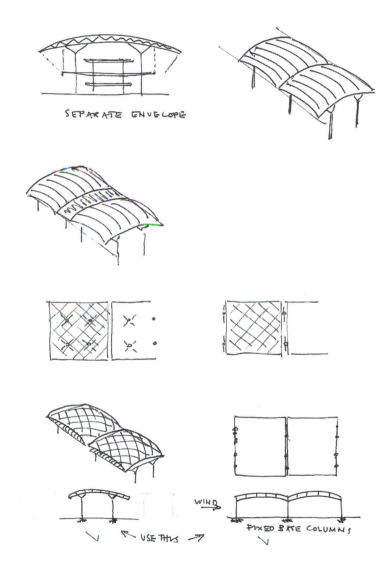

SEPARATE ENVELOPE

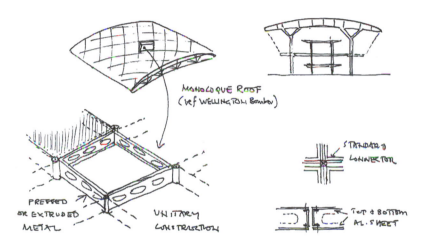

MONOCOQUE ROOF
(ref WELLINGTON Bomber)

PRESSED
OR EXTRUDED
METAL

UNITARY
CONSTRUCTION

STANDARD
CONNECTOR

TOP & BOTTOM
AL. SHEET

WIND

← USE THIS →

FIXED BASE COLUMNS

71

Terminal 5 Heathrow, London

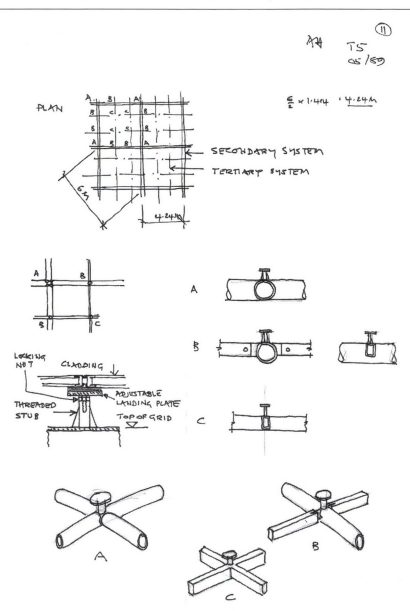

AA TS
⑪
05/89

$\frac{6}{2} \times 1.414 = 4.24m$

PLAN

SECONDARY SYSTEM

TERTIARY SYSTEM

6m

4.24m

A B A
B C C B
B C C B
A B B A

LOCKING
NUT

CLADDING ↓

ADJUSTABLE
LANDING PLATE

THREADED
STUB

TOP OF GRID
▽

A   B   C

ROOF CLADDING

DIAGRID SECONDARY SYSTEM

DIAGRID TERTIARY SYSTEM FORMING 9 SQUARES
WITHIN SECONDARY SYSTEM TO SUPPORT CLADDING

CLADDING FRAME SUPPORTED ON ADJUSTABLE HEIGHT
STOOLS (ALL STOOLS IDENTICAL)

Job: Akropolis Museum, Athens

Client: City of Athens

Architect: Future Systems

Date: 1989 – Competition entry

- Brief – three possible sites for proposed building
- Visit by architect and engineer determined which site to choose
- Initial sketch design produced in café adjacent to site, on a paper napkin
- Idea – to produce a diaphanous envelope over layers of exhibition space
- Vierendeel diagrid curved roof with glazing of varying density supported on concrete perimeter 'berm'
- In situ reinforced concrete frame supported on a raft
- Ribbon bridge linking museum to Akropolis hill – pre-stressed cables supporting a precast concrete deck

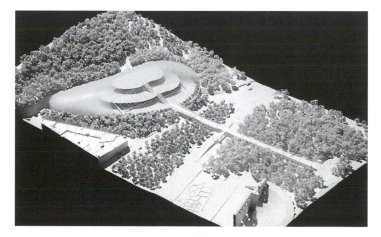

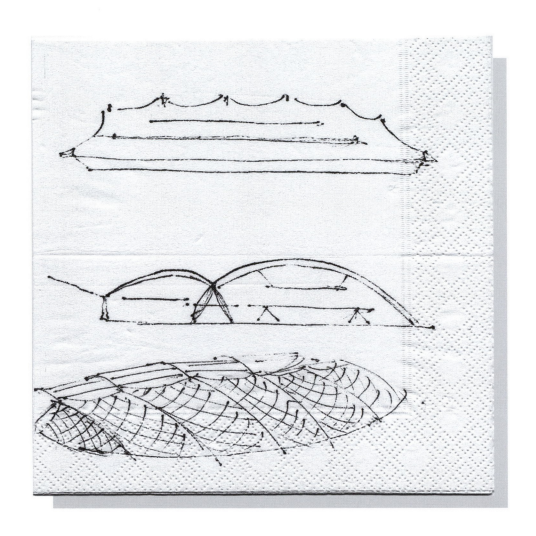

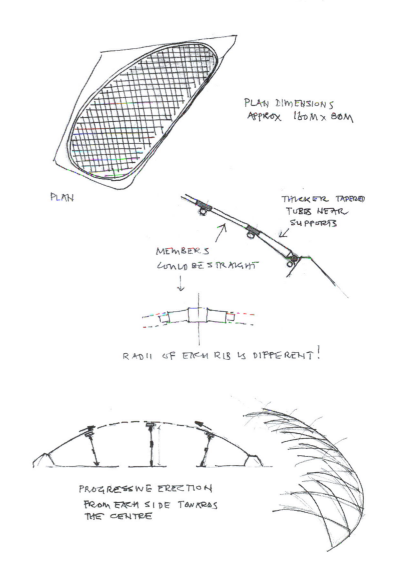

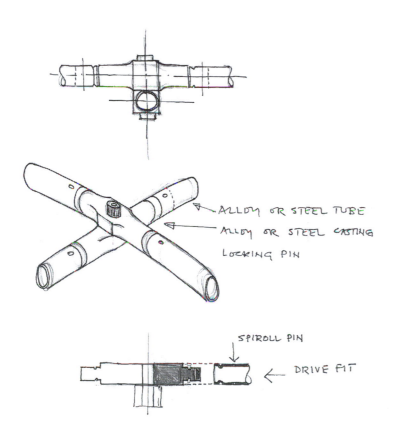

AKROPOLIS MUSEUM 11/89 AH.

PLAN DIMENSIONS
APPROX 150M X 80M

PLAN

THICKER TAPERED
TUBES NEAR
SUPPORTS

MEMBERS
COULD BE STRAIGHT

RADII OF EACH RIB IS DIFFERENT!

PROGRESSIVE ERECTION
FROM EACH SIDE TOWARDS
THE CENTRE

ALLOY OR STEEL TUBE

ALLOY OR STEEL CASTING

LOCKING PIN

SPIROLL PIN

← DRIVE FIT

TUBES : SQUARE OR CIRCULAR
(mainly compression, some bending
Due to local loading).

Akropolis Museum, Athens

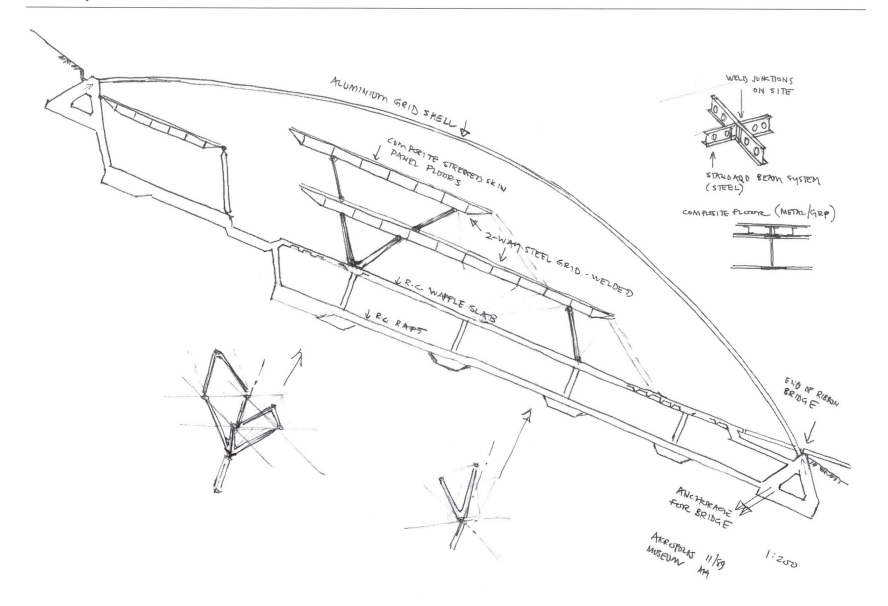

ALUMINIUM GRID SHELL

WELD JUNCTIONS ON SITE

STANDARD BEAM SYSTEM (STEEL)

COMPOSITE FLOOR (METAL/GRP)

COMPOSITE STRESSED SKIN PANEL FLOORS

2-WAY STEEL GRID - WELDED

R.C WAFFLE SLAB

R.C RAFT

END OF RIBBON BRIDGE

ANCHORAGE FOR BRIDGE

AKROPOLIS MUSEUM AA   11/89   1:250

Law Faculty

Job: Law Faculty, Cambridge

Client: University of Cambridge

Architect: Foster Associates

Date: 1990 – Built

- Sensitive site – garden with ancient walnut tree
- Complex brief
- Idea – stepped back floors with minimum supports covered with glazed vault structure preferably unsupported by internal structure
- Part precast part in situ concrete main structure with reinforced concrete cores and raking columns
- Vault structure as diagonal vierendeel lattice supporting part double-glazed and part opaque cladding system
- Diagonal end wall with slender, specially fabricated steel mullions

Law Faculty, Cambridge

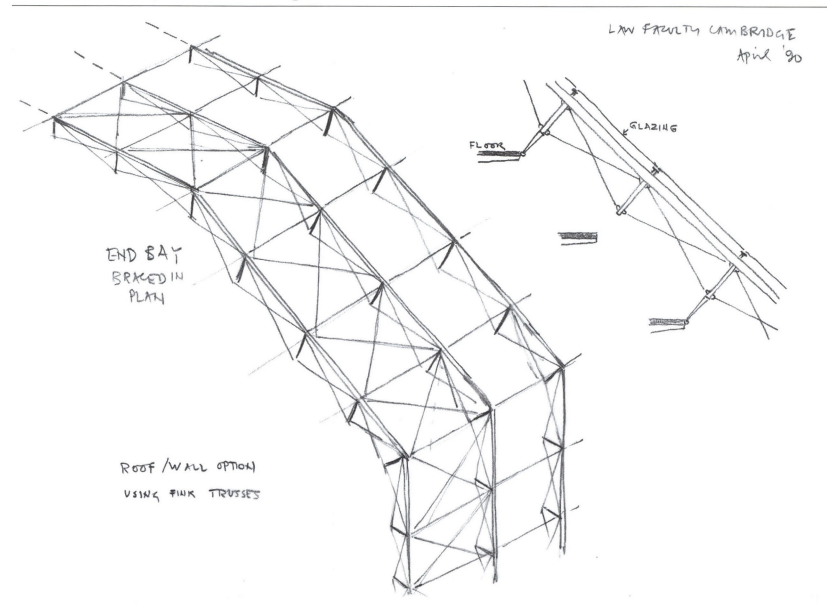

END BAY
BRACED IN
PLAN

ROOF/WALL OPTION
USING FINK TRUSSES

LAW FACULTY CAMBRIDGE
April '90

FLOOR

GLAZING

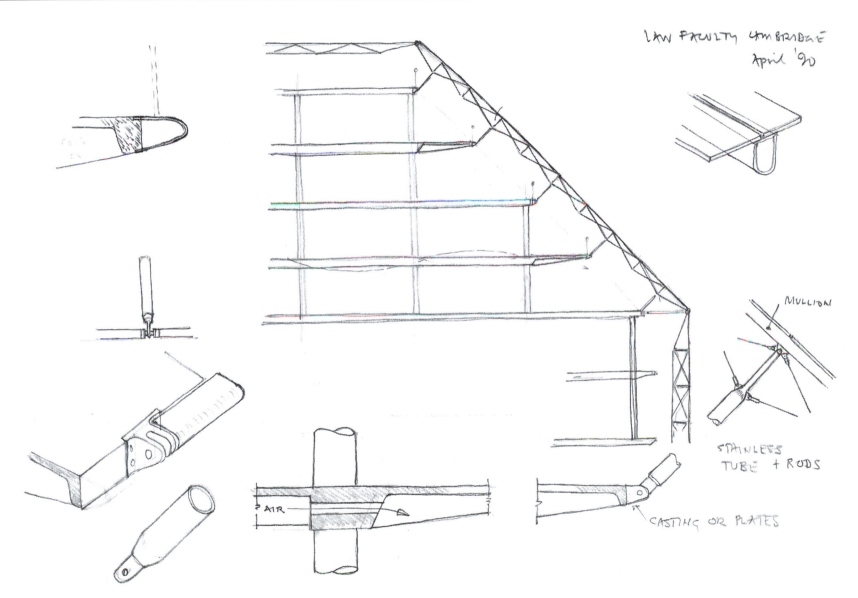

LAW FACULTY CAMBRIDGE
April '90

MULLION

STAINLESS
TUBE + RODS

AIR

CASTING OR PLATES

Law Faculty, Cambridge

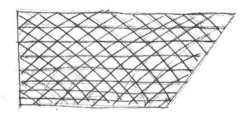

PLAN — 3-WAY STRUCTURE

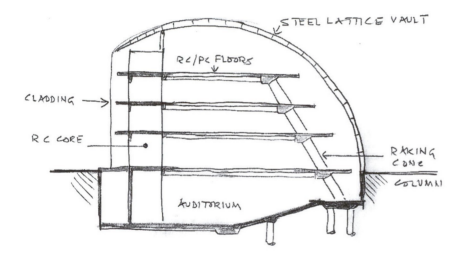

STEEL LATTICE VAULT

RC/PC FLOORS

CLADDING

RC CORE

RAKING CONE

COLUMN

AUDITORIUM

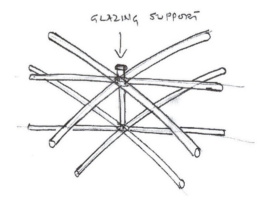

GLAZING SUPPORT

3-WAY VIERENDEEL JOINT

Centre des Conférences Internationale

Paris

Job: Centre des Conférences
Internationale, Paris
'Les Boîtes de Verre'

Client: French Government

Architect: Francis Soler

Date: 1990 – Competition winner, unbuilt

- Brief – to design three similar glass box enclosures, the biggest in the world
- The architect specified that no structural elements could be latticed and there was to be no diagonal bracing
- All four walls and the roof fully glazed with a double system of outer and inner layers 3m apart
- Primary structure developed as an in-plane vierendeel for walls and roof on inner plane
- Secondary structure projects from inner plane to support outer glazing
- Sophisticated cast steel bracket system developed to support cladding
- Full size mock-ups built for testing

Centre des Conférences Internationale, Paris

LES BÔITES DE VERRE 1.
6/90

PRINCIPLES 2
6/90

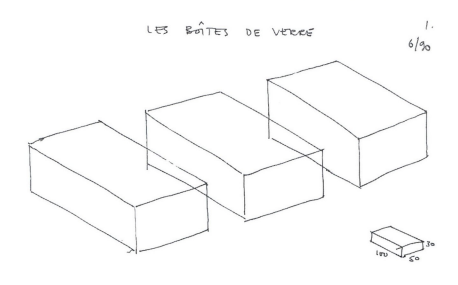

100 50 30

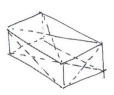

5 PLANES - EACH MUST BE RIGID
IN ITSELF

THE GLASS CANNOT CONTRIBUTE
TO RIGIDITY - IT MUST FLOAT
ON THE STRUCTURE THEREFORE :-

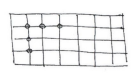

THE STRUCTURE COULD USE
STIFF JOINTS

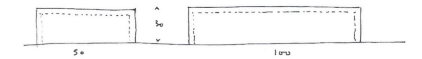

50   100   30

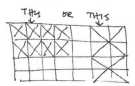

THIS OR THIS

USE DIAGONAL BRACING
TO PANELS, SMALL GRID
OR MEDIUM GRID

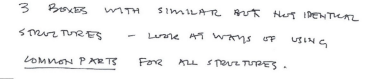

3 BOXES WITH SIMILAR BUT NOT IDENTICAL
STRUCTURES - LOOK AT WAYS OF USING
COMMON PARTS FOR ALL STRUCTURES.

OR

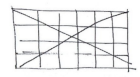

1 BRACED PANEL.

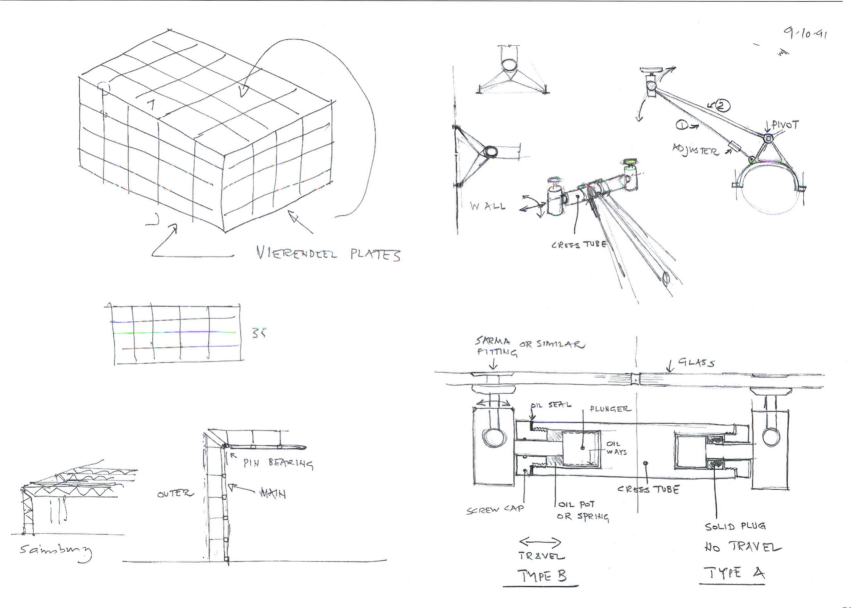

9·10·91

VIERENDEEL PLATES

WALL

CROSS TUBE

ADJUSTER

PIVOT

35

PIN BEARING

OUTER

MAIN

Sainsbury

SARMA OR SIMILAR
FITTING

GLASS

OIL SEAL

PLUNGER

OIL WAYS

CROSS TUBE

SCREW CAP

OIL POT
OR SPRING

SOLID PLUG

NO TRAVEL

TYPE A

TRAVEL

TYPE B

Centre des Conférences Internationale, Paris

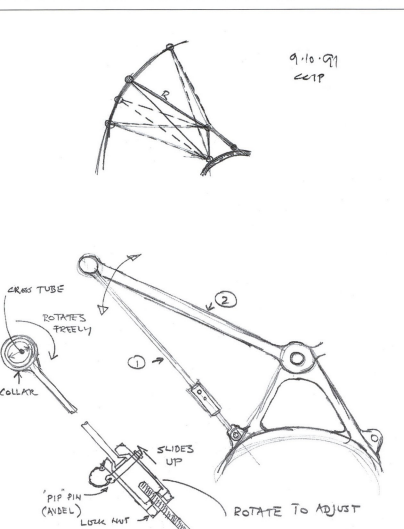

9.10.91
CWP

CROSS TUBE

ROTATES
FREELY

COLLAR

②

①

SLIDES
UP

'PIP' PIN
(AVDEL)

LOCK NUT

ROTATE TO ADJUST

XRM ①

Job: 'Big Roof' Arena,
London Docklands

Client: LDDC

Architect: Avery Associates

Date: 1991 – Unbuilt project

- Ideas for covering a big non-rectangular space between two banks of perimeter buildings
- Best solution seemed to be a series of inflated dirigibles linked together to form a zero weight roof

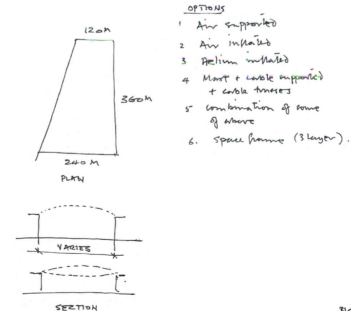

OPTIONS

1. Air supported
2. Air inflated
3. Helium inflated
4. Mast + cable supported + cable trusses
5. combination of some of above
6. space frame (3 layer).

120m

360m

240 M

PLAN

VARIES

SECTION

BIG ROOF ① May 91 AA

'Big Roof' Arena, London Docklands

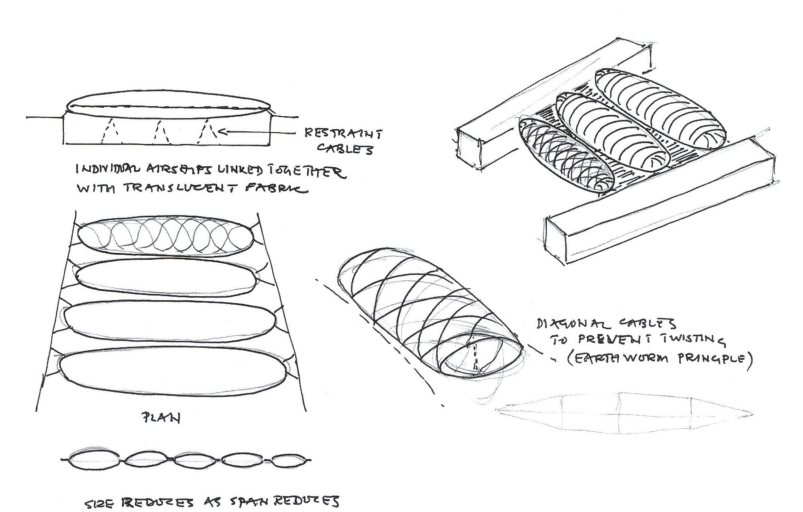

RESTRAINT CABLES

INDIVIDUAL AIRSHIPS LINKED TOGETHER
WITH TRANSLUCENT FABRIC

PLAN

SIZE REDUCES AS SPAN REDUCES

DIAGONAL CABLES
TO PREVENT TWISTING
(EARTHWORM PRINCIPLE)

BIG ROOF 4   May 91   AH.

'Landmark' HQ Building

Job: 'Landmark' HQ Building, Brno

Client: City of Brno/Bovis

Architect: Future Systems

Date: 1992 – Unbuilt project

- Project for a low energy multi-storey office building
- Alternative steel or RC frame and floors
- Steel gridshell roof structure fully glazed providing enclosure to the working floors and forming an atrium internal space

---

BRNO – LANDMARK BUILDING   18·12·92.

PRELIMINARY STRUCTURAL IDEAS

1. SUBSTRUCTURE (DEPENDENT ON SOIL INVESTIGATION)

   ALTERNATIVES
   a) REINFORCED CONCRETE RAFT
   b) CONTINUOUS R.C. BEAM SPREADERS ON COLUMN
      LINES WITH SLAB TIED IN.

2. SUPERSTRUCTURE

   ALTERNATIVES
   a) REINFORCED CONCRETE COLUMN & BEAM FRAME
      WITH INSITU P.C. FLOORS
   b) R.C. COLUMNS WITH INSITU FLAT SLABS
   c) STEEL FRAME WITH PRECAST FLOORS
   d) STEEL FRAME WITH COMPOSITE FLOORS

3. ROOF DOME
   ALTERNATIVES
   a) GRIDSHELL WITH VIERENDEEL STEEL TUBES
      IN UPPER & LOWER PLANES.
   b) FISCHER SYSTEM DOME

EXTRA
 * ——— c) Air-Supported Cable / Hess laphon

4. STABILITY
   COMBINATION OF FRAME ACTION & PLAN CURVATURE

5. THERMAL MOVEMENT
   ALTERNATIVES TO BE EXPLORED.

'Landmark' HQ Building, Brno

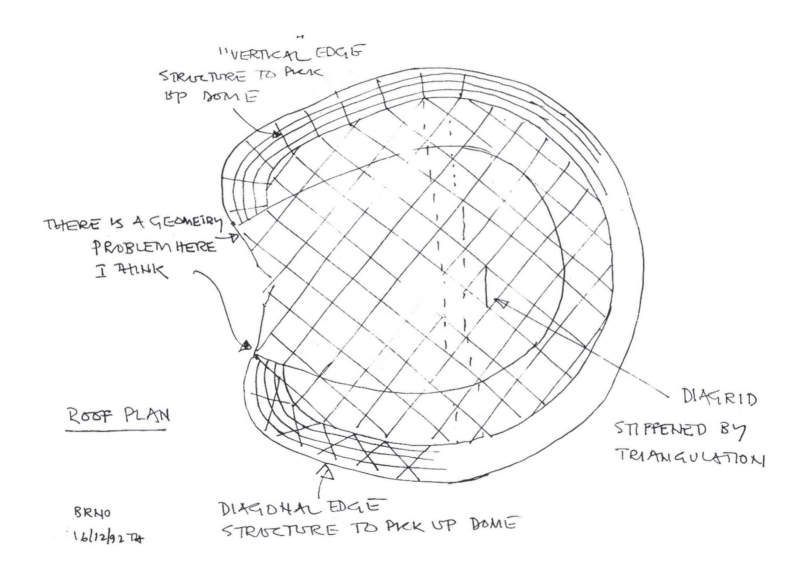

"VERTICAL EDGE
STRUCTURE TO PICK
UP DOME

THERE IS A GEOMETRY
PROBLEM HERE
I THINK

ROOF PLAN

DIAGRID
STIFFENED BY
TRIANGULATION

DIAGONAL EDGE
STRUCTURE TO PICK UP DOME

BRNO
16/12/92 TF

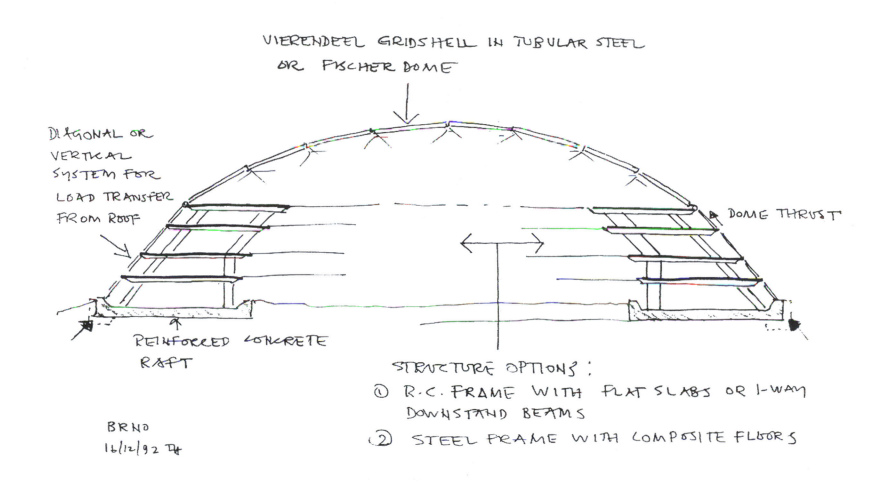

VIERENDEEL GRIDSHELL IN TUBULAR STEEL OR FISCHER DOME

DIAGONAL OR VERTICAL SYSTEM FOR LOAD TRANSFER FROM ROOF

DOME THRUST

REINFORCED CONCRETE RAFT

BRNO
16/12/92 TH

STRUCTURE OPTIONS:
① R.C. FRAME WITH FLAT SLABS OR 1-WAY DOWNSTAND BEAMS
② STEEL FRAME WITH COMPOSITE FLOORS

'Landmark' HQ Building, Brno

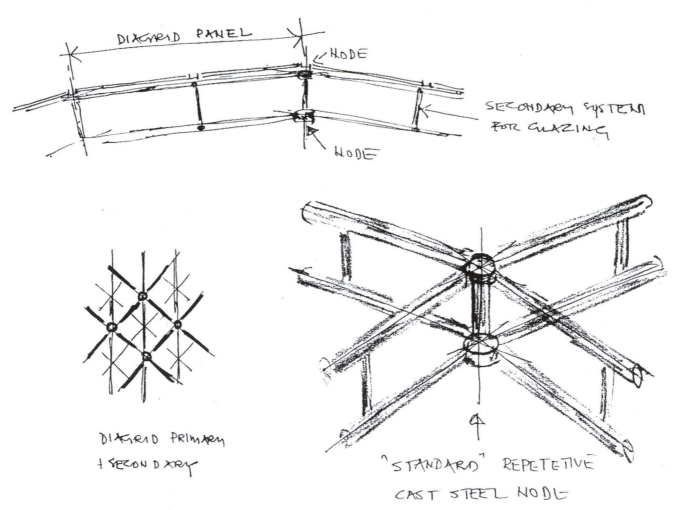

DIAGRID PANEL

NODE

NODE

SECONDARY SYSTEM
FOR GLAZING

DIAGRID PRIMARY
+ SECONDARY

"STANDARD" REPETETIVE
CAST STEEL NODE

BRNO
16/12/92 TA

Croydon Bridge

Job: Croydon Bridge

Client: Borough of Croydon

Architect: Future Systems

Date: 1993 – Unbuilt project

- Pedestrian bridge to span over four-lane highway
- Composite deck beam curved on plan part steel part concrete for mass to damp dynamic behaviour
- Tubular steel inclined main mast with rod tension hangers and back stays to support deck

Croydon Bridge

LOAD CONDITIONS   CROYDON BRIDGE   June '93

DECK

BENDING

ARCHING

TORSION

DYNAMIC FREQUENCY

THERMAL MOVEMENT

AERODYNAMICS

TENSION HANGERS

ELONGATION

THERMAL

AERODYNAMIC / VORTEX SHEDDING

FATIGUE

MAST

COMPRESSION

BENDING

SHORTENING

THERMAL

CAMBER / WATER RUN-OFF

NON SLIP

LOW MAINTENANCE

MAST SECTIONS

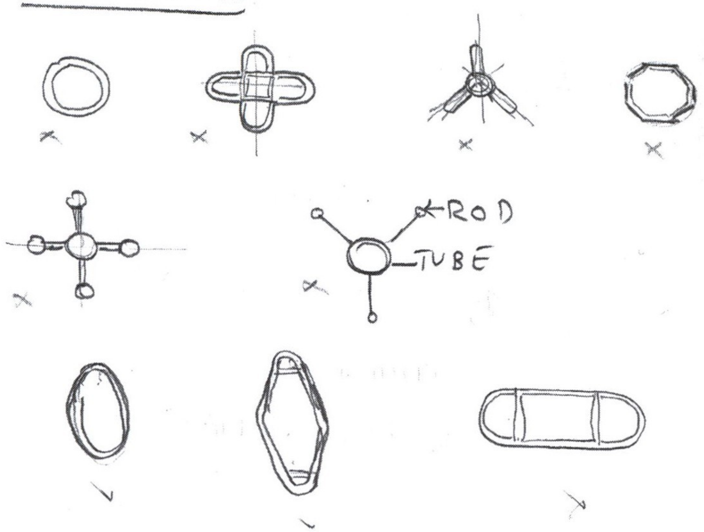

ROD

TUBE

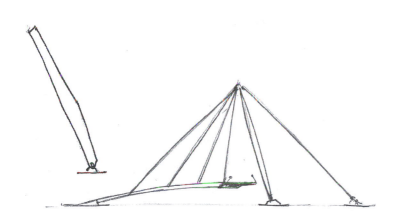

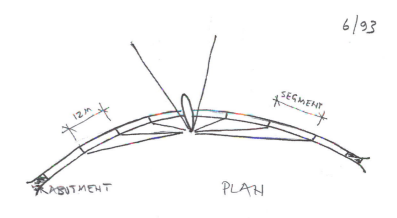

6/93

PLAN

LENGTH — 100 M SAY.

2 × 3 M FOR ABUTMENTS

∴ 96 M BRIDGE LENGTH

8 SEGMENTS   96 ÷ 8 = 12M EACH.

Croydon Bridge

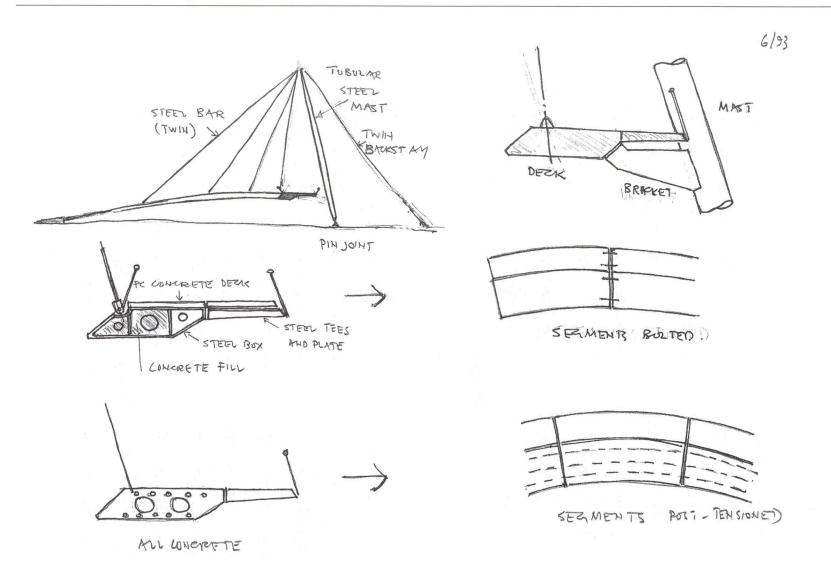

6/93

TUBULAR STEEL MAST

STEEL BAR (TWIN)

TWIN BACKSTAY

PIN JOINT

MAST

DECK

BRACKET

PC CONCRETE DECK

STEEL TEES AND PLATE

STEEL BOX

CONCRETE FILL

SEGMENT BOLTED !

ALL CONCRETE

SEGMENTS POST - TENSIONED

Villepinte Exhibition Halls

Job: Villepinte Exhibition Halls, Paris

Architect: Foster Associates

Date: 1993 – Competition entry, unbuilt

- Very large exhibition hall as extension to existing halls
- Large column spacing required
- Alternative options based on a square repetitive module for design flexibility
- Various vault-type roof structures explored with or without masts and tension assistance
- Domed gridshell steel roof structures proposed with cables to provide hoop tension and 'tree' columns to minimise obstruction at floor level

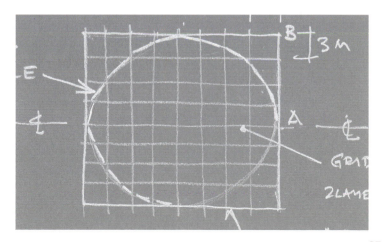

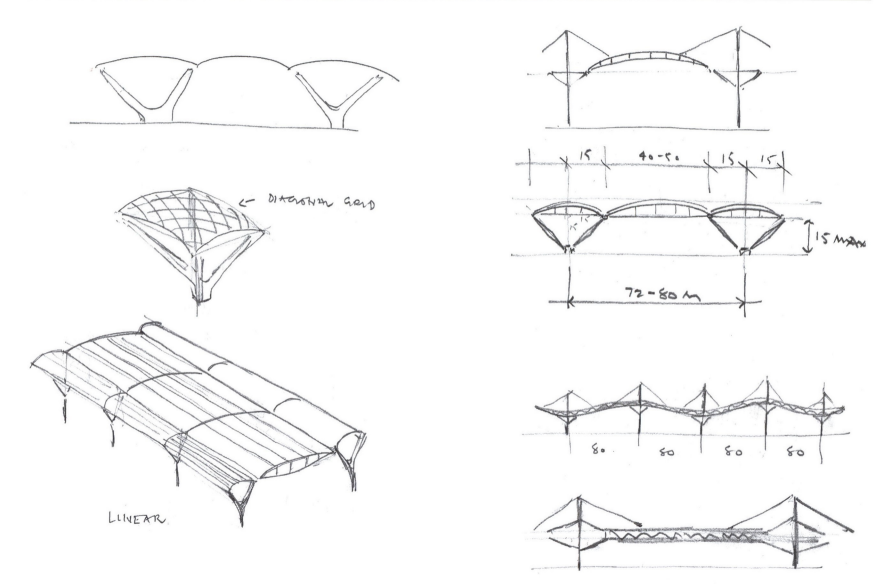

← DIAGONAL GRID

LINEAR

15 | 40-50 | 15 | 15

15 max

72-80 m

80 | 80 | 80 | 80

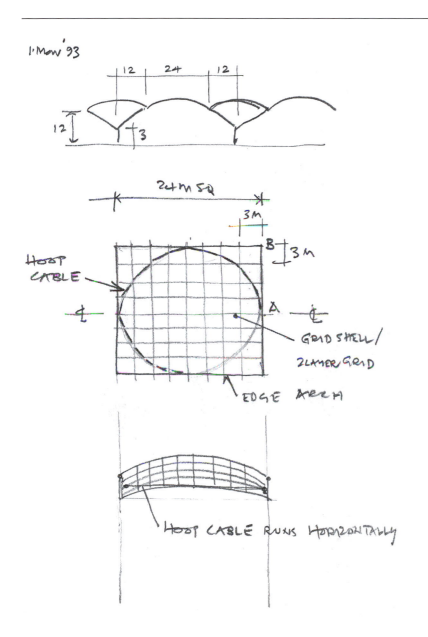

I Mon '93

12 | 24 | 12

12 ↑3

24m SQ

3m

B ↑3m

HOOP CABLE

℄

A ℄

GRID SHELL / 2 LAYER GRID

EDGE ARCH

HOOP CABLE RUNS HORIZONTALLY

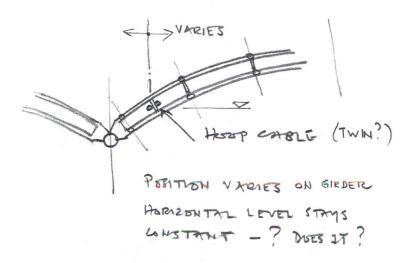

VARIES

HOOP CABLE (TWIN?)

POSITION VARIES ON GIRDER
HORIZONTAL LEVEL STAYS
CONSTANT — ? DOES IT?

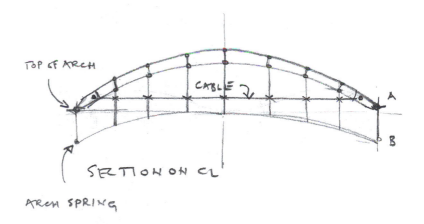

TOP OF ARCH

CABLE

A

B

SECTION ON CL

ARCH SPRING

Hamburg Office

Job: Hamburg Office

Client: City of Hamburg

Architect: Future Systems

Date: 1993 – Competition entry, unbuilt

- Aim – to design an energy efficient building
- Floors of steel hollow box construction water-filled for fireproofing and thermal mass
- Hollow steel columns also water-filled forming circulation system
- Steel two-layer gridshell roof

Hamburg Office

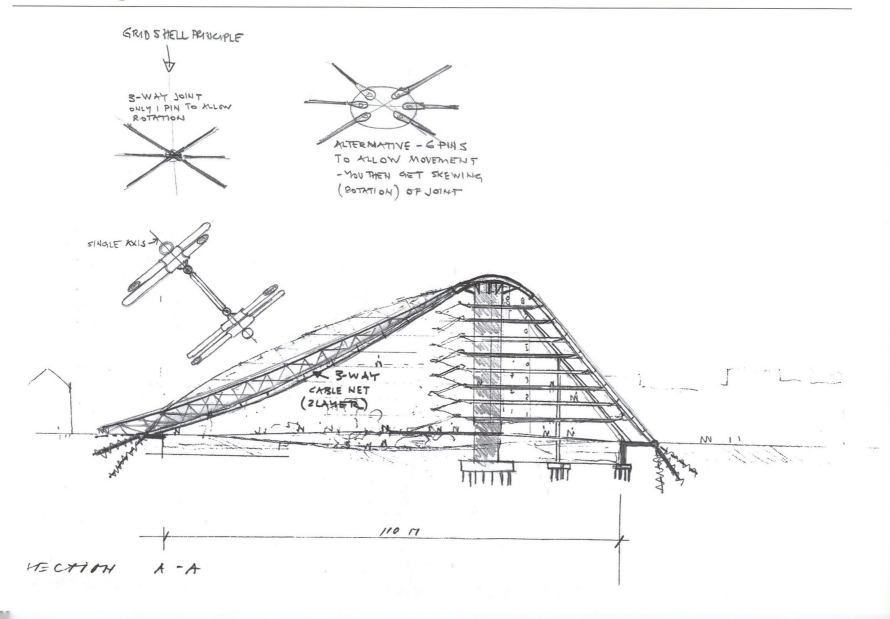

GRID SHELL PRINCIPLE

3-WAY JOINT
ONLY 1 PIN TO ALLOW
ROTATION

ALTERNATIVE - 6 PINS
TO ALLOW MOVEMENT
- YOU THEN GET SKEWING
(ROTATION) OF JOINT

SINGLE AXIS

3-WAY
CABLE NET
(2 LAYER)

110 M

SECTION A-A

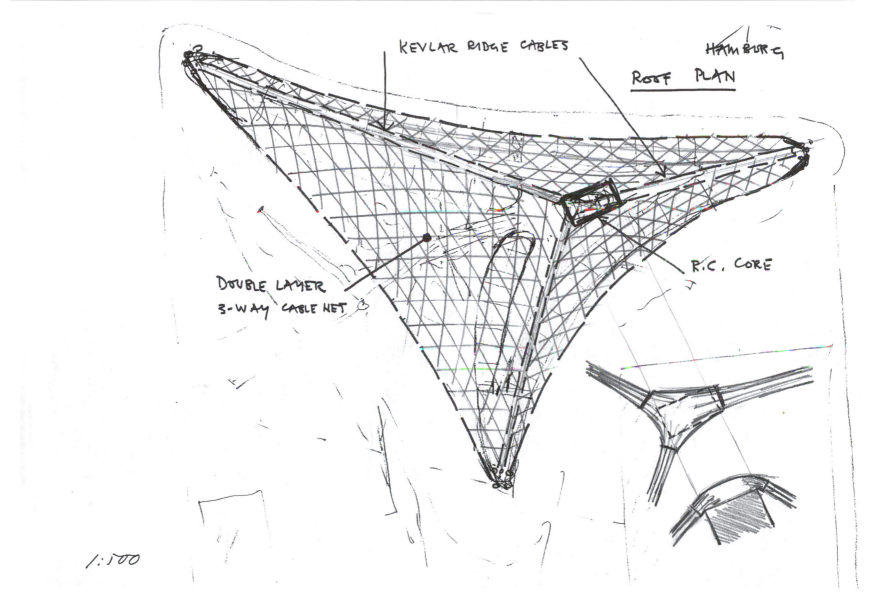

KEVLAR RIDGE CABLES

HAMBURG

ROOF PLAN

R.C. CORE

DOUBLE LAYER
3-WAY CABLE NET

1:500

Merthyr Tydfil Bridge

Job: Merthyr Tydfil Bridge, Wales

Client: Merthyr Tydfil Borough Council

Designer: Tony Hunt

Date: 1994 – Competition

- The brief was to design an enclosure for an existing pedestrian bridge across a highway
- The existing bridge consisted of two lattice steel girders supporting a deck
- The proposal was to add a series of perforated steel hoops supporting stainless steel side panels and a Teflon/glass fabric roof
- Support columns were also clad in stainless steel sheet
- Downlighting was incorporated in new handrails and uplighting to the fabric roof

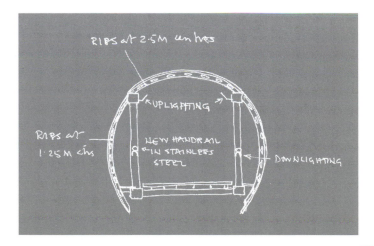

Merthyr Tydfil Bridge, Wales

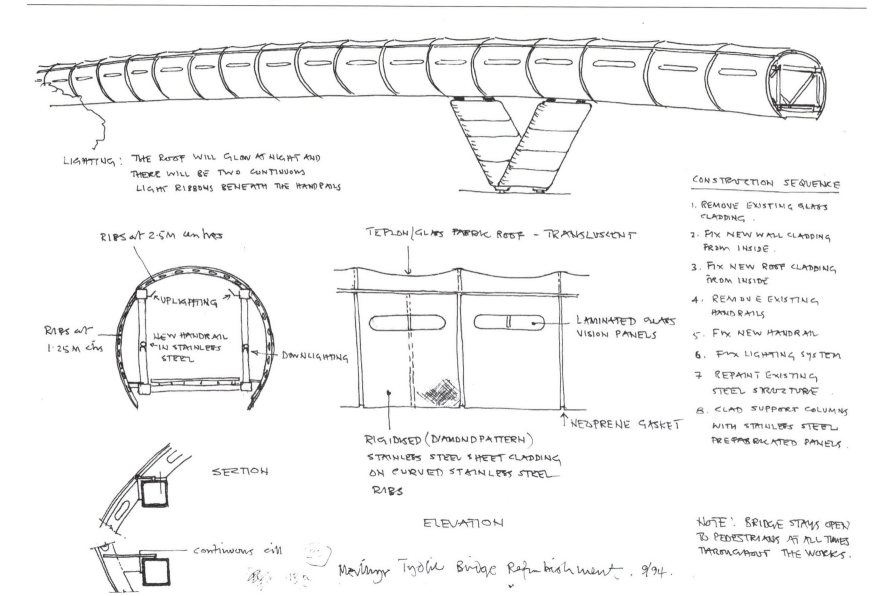

LIGHTING: THE ROOF WILL GLOW AT NIGHT AND THERE WILL BE TWO CONTINUOUS LIGHT RIBBONS BENEATH THE HANDRAILS

RIBS AT 2.5M centres

↗ UPLIGHTING

NEW HANDRAIL IN STAINLESS STEEL

RIBS AT 1.25M ctrs

DOWNLIGHTING

SECTION

continuous cill

TEFLON/GLASS FABRIC ROOF - TRANSLUCENT

LAMINATED GLASS VISION PANELS

↑ NEOPRENE GASKET

RIGIDISED (DIAMOND PATTERN) STAINLESS STEEL SHEET CLADDING ON CURVED STAINLESS STEEL RIBS

ELEVATION

Merthyr Tydfil Bridge Refurbishment. 9/94.

CONSTRUCTION SEQUENCE

1. REMOVE EXISTING GLASS CLADDING.

2. FIX NEW WALL CLADDING FROM INSIDE.

3. FIX NEW ROOF CLADDING FROM INSIDE

4. REMOVE EXISTING HANDRAILS

5. FIX NEW HANDRAIL

6. FIX LIGHTING SYSTEM

7. REPAINT EXISTING STEEL STRUCTURE

8. CLAD SUPPORT COLUMNS WITH STAINLESS STEEL PREFABRICATED PANELS.

NOTE: BRIDGE STAYS OPEN TO PEDESTRIANS AT ALL TIMES THROUGHOUT THE WORKS.

West India Quay Bridge

Job: West India Quay Bridge,
             London Docklands

Client: LDDC

Architect: Future Systems

Date: 1994 – Built

- Initial discussion with the architects
  – a mast and cable bridge –
  immediately rejected as restless and
  not what we felt appropriate
- Floating pontoon bridge suggested
  and sketched – brilliant idea
- Geometry developed
- Vertical deflexions under live load a
  problem to be solved – it is a series
  of boats!
- Horizontal drift under wind also
  a problem
- Basic concept followed through
  from day one – unusual!
- Tension piles solve deflexion and
  drift problems

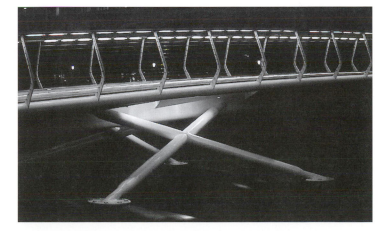

West India Quay Bridge, London Docklands

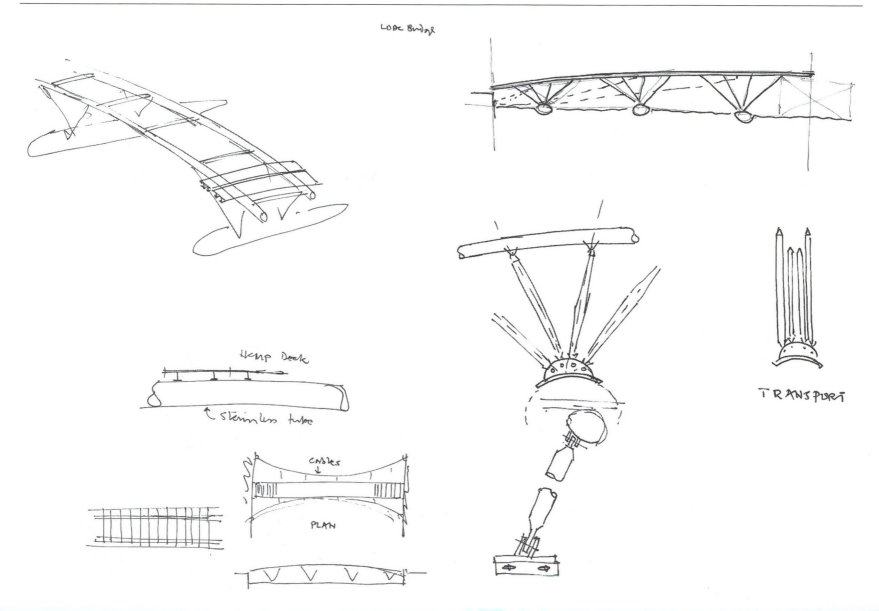

LDDC Bridge

Hemp Deck

↑ Stainless tube

cables

PLAN

TRANSPORT

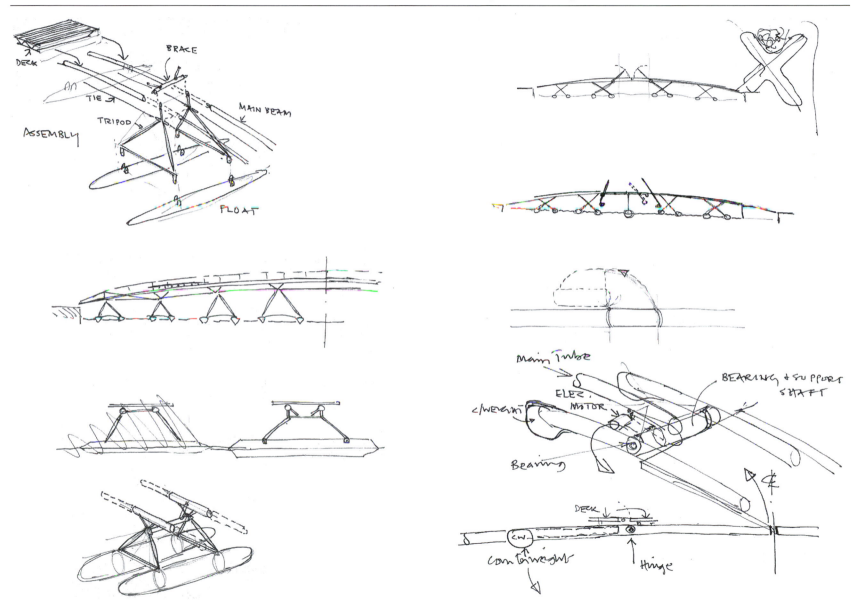

Stonehenge Visitor Centre

Job: Stonehenge Visitor Centre

Client: UK Government

Architect: Future Systems

Date: 1994 – Competition entry, unbuilt

- Clear span single storey enclosure with minimum number of columns
- A bubble rising out of the grass
- Glazed view to Stonehenge, grass roof elsewhere
- Tubular beam roof structure with pre-stressed lower tension cables

Stonehenge Visitor Centre

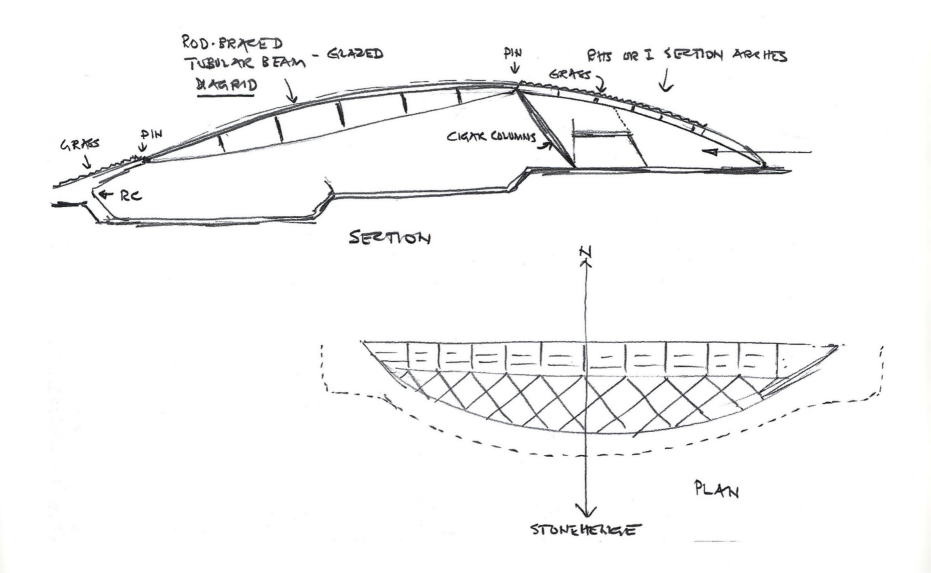

ROD·BRACED TUBULAR BEAM - GLAZED DIAGRID

PIN

PITS OR I SECTION ARCHES

GRASS

GRASS

PIN

CIGAR COLUMNS

RC

SECTION

N

PLAN

STONEHENGE

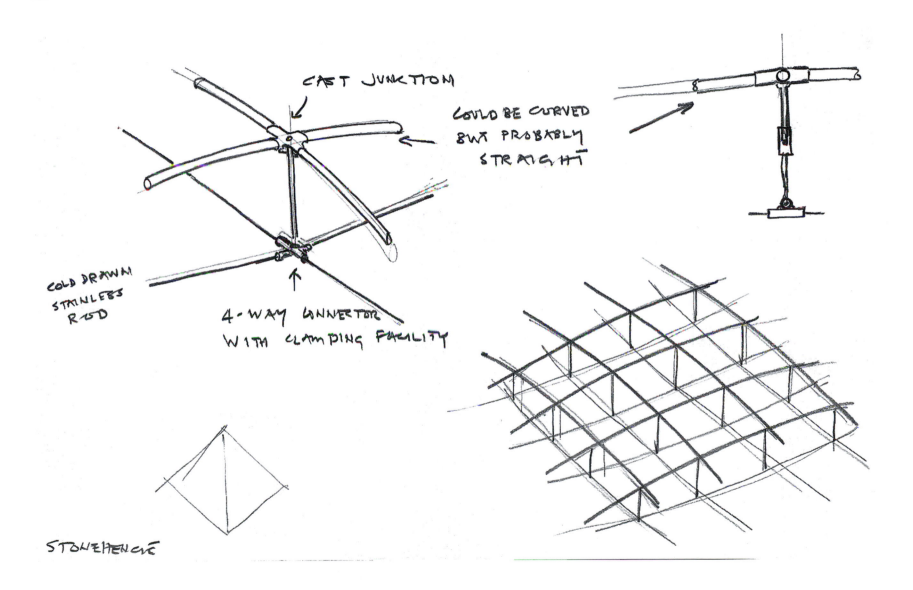

CAST JUNCTION

COULD BE CURVED
BUT PROBABLY
STRAIGHT

COLD DRAWN
STAINLESS
ROD

4-WAY CONNECTOR
WITH CLAMPING FACILITY

STONEHENGE

National Botanic Garden of Wales

Job: National Botanic Garden of Wales

Client: National Botanic Garden of Wales

Architect: Foster and Partners

Date: 1995 – Built

- First conversation – should it be a linear vault, a dome or a toroid
- Could we make the structure a single layer rather than a two-layer vierendeel (Cambridge Law Faculty)
- Sketches and rough calculations – probably achievable but concerned about snap through due to out of balance loading with shallow curvature
- Explore diagrid form – proportions are wrong for two-way load sharing
- Develop one-way slender stiffened tubular steel arch structure spanning short direction with orthogonal linking tubes
- Toroidal dome springs from perimeter concrete ring buried beneath grassed landscape

Dome

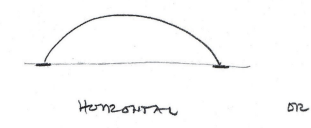

HORIZONTAL   OR

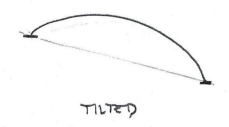

TILTED

CAN BE CIRCULAR

OR ELLIPTICAL ∨

VAULT NEEDS

SAME EDGE CONDITIONS

ON LONG SIDES

OUTWARD THRUST TO BE RESISTED

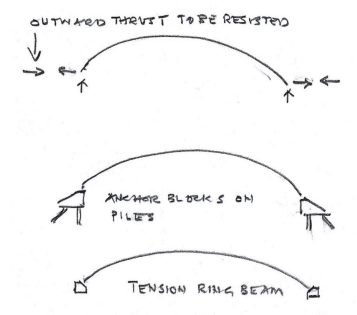

ANCHOR BLOCKS ON PILES

TENSION RING BEAM

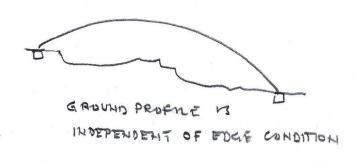

GROUND PROFILE IS
INDEPENDENT OF EDGE CONDITION

Middleton Botanic Garden 3/95

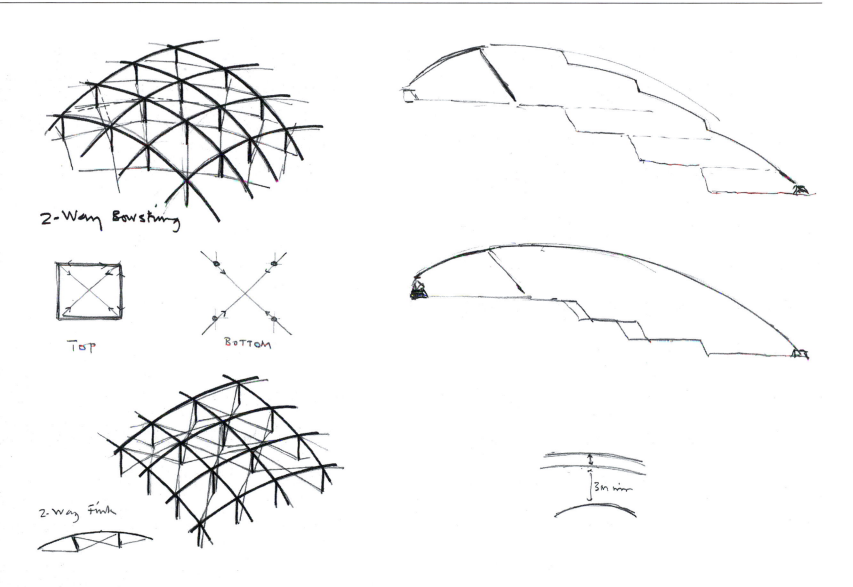

2-Way Bowstring

TOP

BOTTOM

2-Way Fink

3m min

National Botanic Garden of Wales

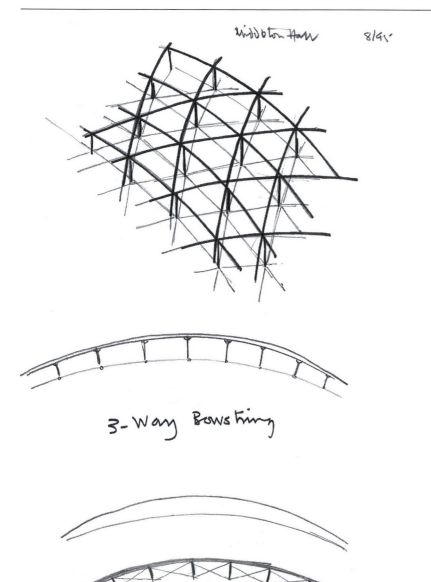

3-Way Bowstring

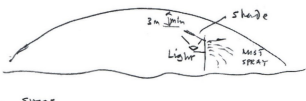

3m 1min   Shade

Light   Mist Spray

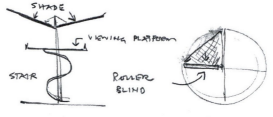

SHADE

VIEWING PLATFORM

STAIR   ROLLER BLIND

Single Layer   or   2 Layer

90° or 60°

Grid of Dome has to provide lines for
Zone dividers

Structural Grid :   Coarse with secondary
glazing structure

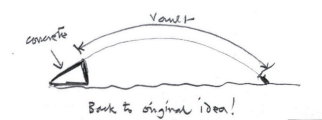

concrete   Vault

Back to original idea!

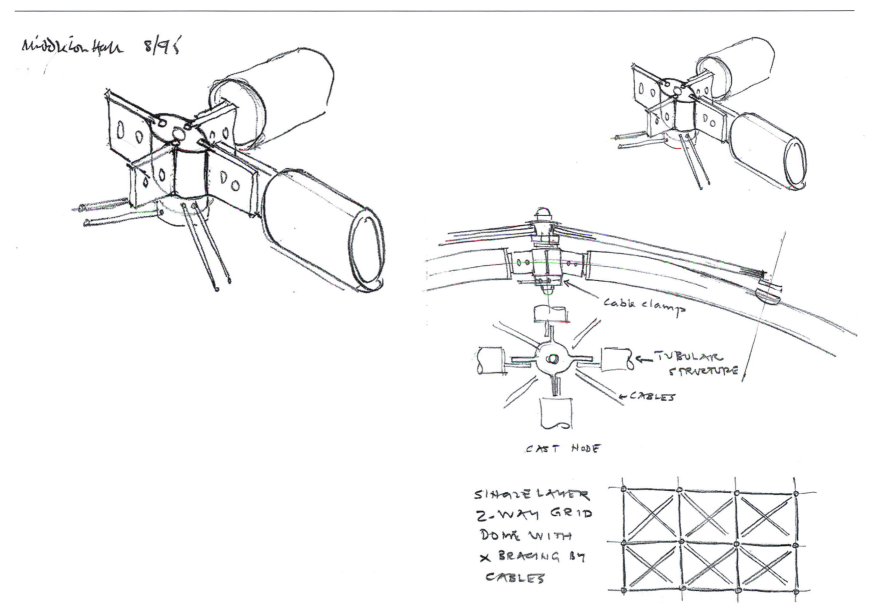

Middleton Hall 8/95

cable clamp

TUBULAR STRUCTURE

← CABLES

CAST NODE

SINGLE LAYER
2-WAY GRID
DOME WITH
X BRACING BY
CABLES

Glass Bridge

Paddington

Job: Glass Bridge, Paddington

Client: Chelsfield plc

Designer: Thomas Heatherwick

Date: 1996–2002 – Ongoing

- The aim was to design and develop an all glass bridge made up from sheets of glass adhesive bonded together with no mechanical fastenings and based on a model by Tom Heatherwick
- Original client-sponsored scheme for a 20 metre bridge was abandoned
- Office research has continued into a full feasibility study
- The new client has approved a revised bridge design of 7 metre span using full length glass panel beams clamped together only at the ends
- The full height glass handrails which are separate from the bridge deck, also span clear between abutments

Glass Bridge, Paddington

GLASS BRIDGE
Nov '98
INITIAL IDEAS

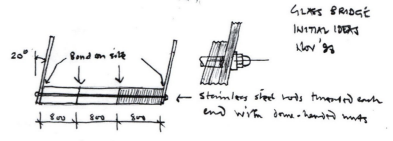

20°   Bond on site

800   800   800

stainless steel rods threaded each
end with dome-headed nuts

Fabricate in 3 separate 800 mm wide section.
Bolt together this providing fail-safe fixing
for handrail which is also adhesive bonded
to outermost leaf of deck.

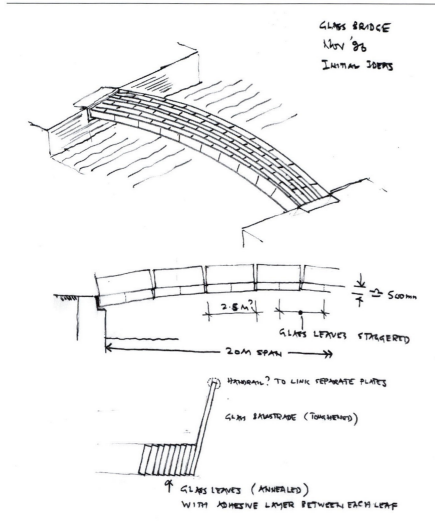

500mm

2.5M ?

GLASS LEAVES STAGGERED

← 20M SPAN →

HANDRAIL? TO LINK SEPARATE PLATES

GLASS BALUSTRADE (TOUGHENED)

9 GLASS LEAVES (ANNEALED)
WITH ADHESIVE LAYER BETWEEN EACH LEAF

BRIDGE ACTS AS 2-PIN ARCH

SPAN - 20M   WIDTH - 2.4M   DEPTH ± 500mm
GLASS PIECE LENGTH - 2.5M   GLASS THICKNESS - 20mm

GLASS BRIDGE
INITIAL IDEAS
Nov '98

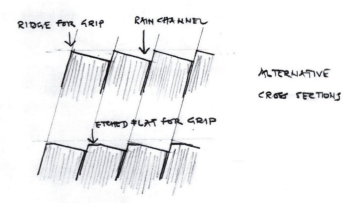

RIDGE FOR GRIP   RAIN CHANNEL

ETCHED FLAT FOR GRIP

ALTERNATIVE
CROSS SECTIONS

Note - Each piece of glass identical except
for ½ length pieces at ends.
∴ only 2 types required.

GLASS BRIDGE

LIGHTING IDEA

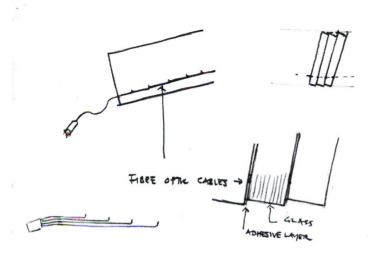

FIBRE OPTIC CABLES →

GLASS

ADHESIVE LAYER

PHOTO ELASTIC BEHAVIOUR UNDER VARYING LIVE LOAD
COULD ALTER COLOUR? OR DICHROIC LIGHT SOURCES

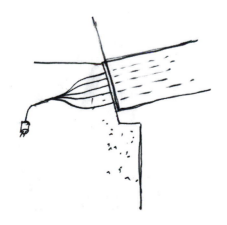

'Gigaworld'

Kuala Lumpur

Job: 'Gigaworld', Kuala Lumpur

Client: K L Linear City Sdn Bhd

Architect: Jimmy Loh for Linear City

Date: 1996 – Project abandoned

- Part of a proposed 12 km 'Linear City' to be built over the river Klang running through the centre of Kuala Lumpur. This section 1.8 km long
- Building has to be elevated above river to leave it open and accessible to the city
- A multi-storey reinforced concrete structure with a hull structure spanning between access tower columns
- Main hull building interspersed with 40 storey towers for offices/hotels/apartments
- Complex construction sequence devised for fabrication of 'hull' sections from which the rest of the structure springs
- Canal to be formed at an intermediate level
- Retractable fabric roof shading structures

'Gigaworld', Kuala Lumpur

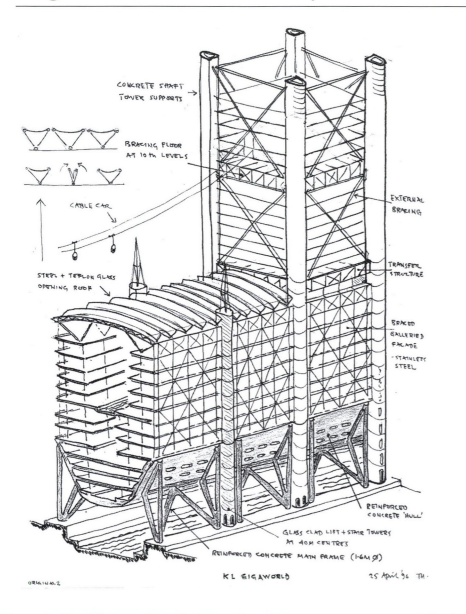

CONCRETE SHAFT TOWER SUPPORTS

BRACING FLOOR AT 10th LEVELS

CABLE CAR

STEEL + TEFLON GLASS OPENING ROOF

EXTERNAL BRACING

TRANSFER STRUCTURE

BRACED GALLERIED FACADE - STAINLESS STEEL

REINFORCED CONCRETE 'HULL'

GLASS CLAD LIFT + STAIR TOWERS AT 40M CENTRES

REINFORCED CONCRETE MAIN FRAME (1.6M ∅)

K L GIGAWORLD   25 April 96 TH.

ORIGINAL 2

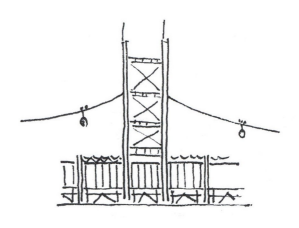

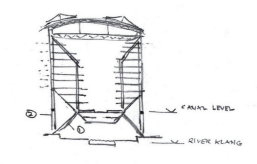

CANAL LEVEL

RIVER KLANG

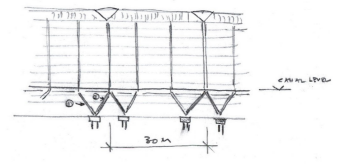

CANAL LEVEL

30 M

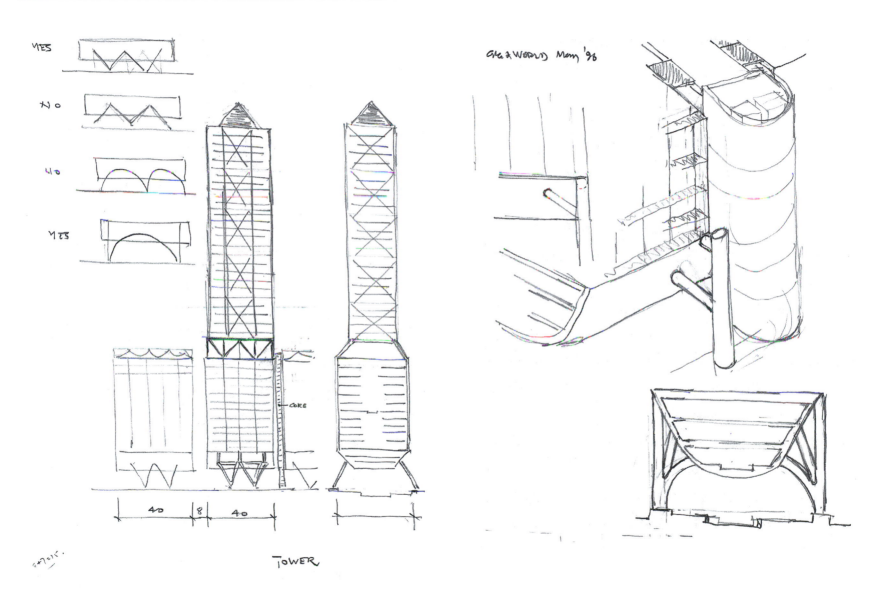

YES

NO

NO

YES

GIGAWORLD May '96

CORE

40 | 8 | 40

TOWER

'Gigaworld', Kuala Lumpur

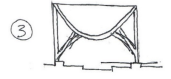 HULL SUPPORT OPTIONS   GIGAWORLD May '88

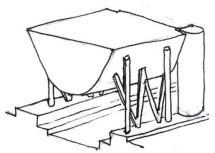 GIGAWORLD May '88

③

④

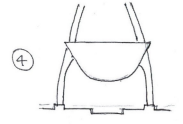

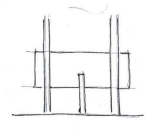

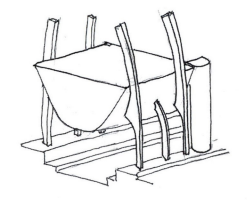

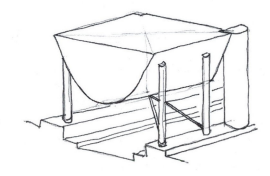

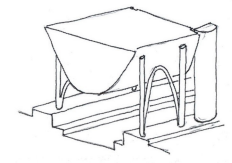

HULL SUPPORT OPTIONS

Gigaworld May 96

OPENING FABRIC ROOFS

PIVOTING HYPAR (X)

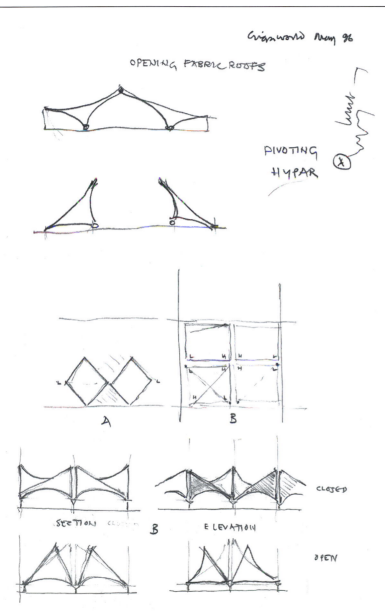

A

B

SECTION   B   ELEVATION   CLOSED

OPEN

Gigaworld May

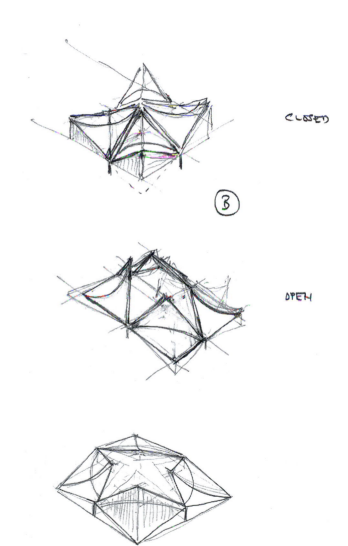

CLOSED

(B)

OPEN

Hungerford Bridge

London

Job: Hungerford Bridge, London

Client: Millennium Project

Architect: Alsop and Störmer

Date: 1996 – Competition entry, unbuilt

- Aim – to produce a pedestrian deck structure above the existing bridge
- Existing bridge cannot accept any further loading
- Span a new deck structure onto edge girders
- Edge girders run alongside existing girders and span directly onto existing caisson piers via twin columns
- Edge girders to be visually as light as possible with no diagonals

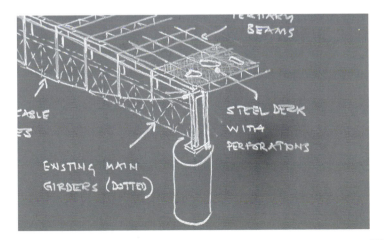

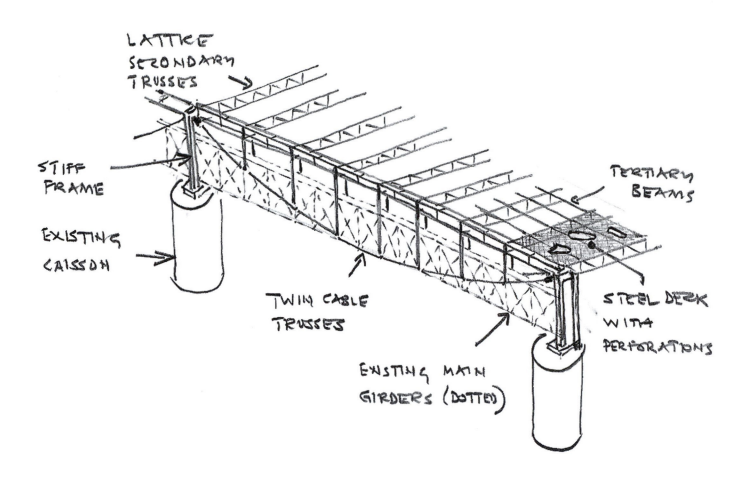

LATTICE
SECONDARY
TRUSSES

STIFF
FRAME

EXISTING
CAISSON

TWIN CABLE
TRUSSES

TERTIARY
BEAMS

STEEL DECK
WITH
PERFORATIONS

EXISTING MAIN
GIRDERS (DOTTED)

HUNGERFORD BRIDGE   8/96

Dyson Appliances

Malmesbury

Job: Dyson Appliances, Malmesbury

Client: James Dyson

Architect: Chris Wilkinson Architects

Date: 1997 – Built

- Aim – economic elegant building for high profile client
- Simple repetitive steel structure capable of extension – now being doubled in size
- Braced 'wave' beams for efficiency supporting long span deep profile deck
- Double height glazed entrance pavilion as link between existing unit and new
- Membrane entrance canopy

Dyson Appliances, Malmesbury

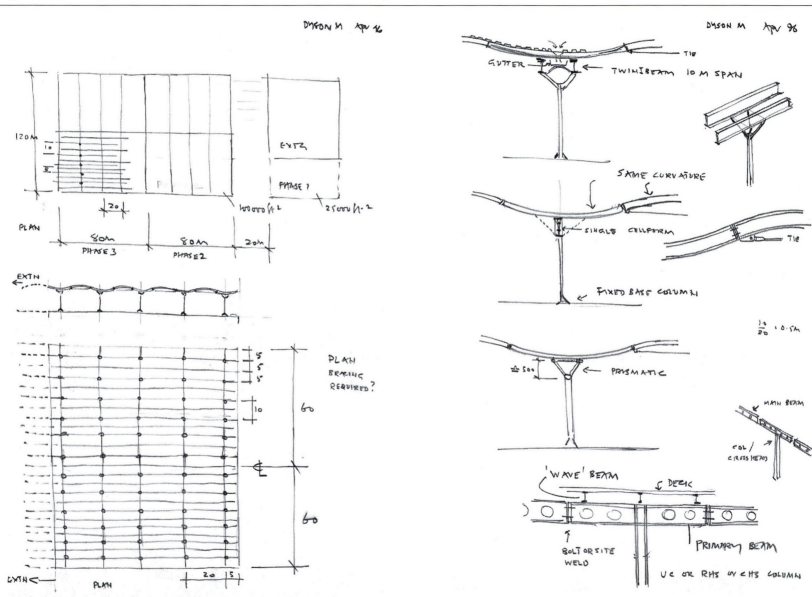

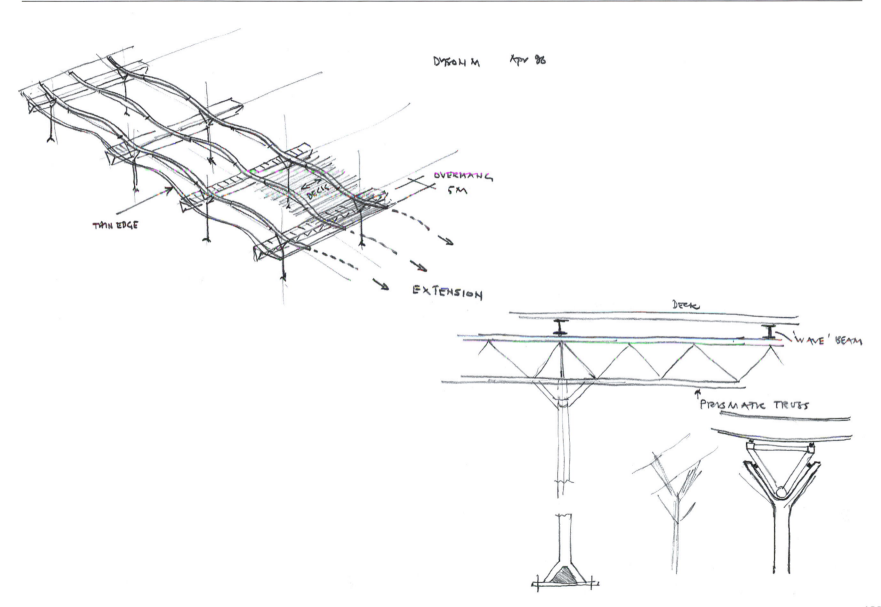

DYSON M   APV 96

OVERHANG
5M

THIN EDGE

DECK

EXTENSION

DECK

'WAVE' BEAM

PRISMATIC TRUSS

Croydon Arena and Hotel Tower

Job: Croydon Arena and Hotel Tower

Client: Arrowcroft

Architect: Michael Aukett Architects

Date: 1987 – Project

- Arena – exploring alternative ways of structuring a large clear span shallow circular dome on an elliptical plan
- Slender cigar shape columns
- Trying solutions other than conventional radial trusses
- Economy and repetition important
- Tower – new ways of supporting and stiffening a slender multi-storey slab/tower

Croydon Arena and Hotel Tower

Croydon Arena 6/97

Roof Ellipse

122 × 107 M to col. centres,

Down to 100 × 85~

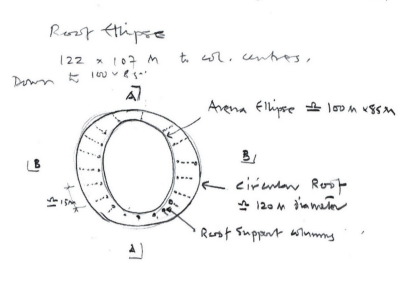

Arena Ellipse ≃ 100 M × 85 M

Circular Roof ≃ 120 M diameter

Roof Support columns

≃ 15M

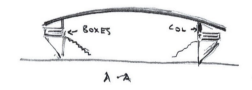

← BOXES   COL →

A - A

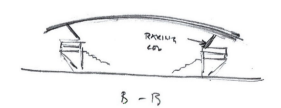

RAKING COL

B - B

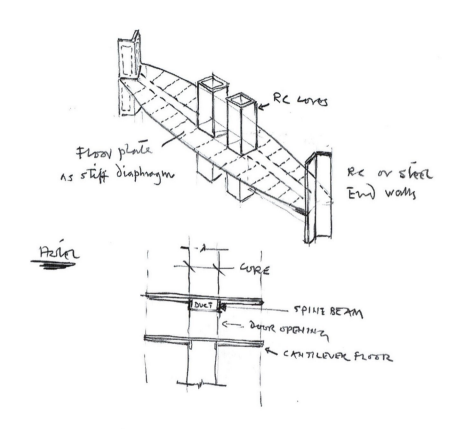

RC cores

Floor plate as stiff diaphragm

RC or steel End walls

CORE

SPINE BEAM

DOOR OPENING

CANTILEVER FLOOR

15/20 STOREY R.C. FRAME TOWER

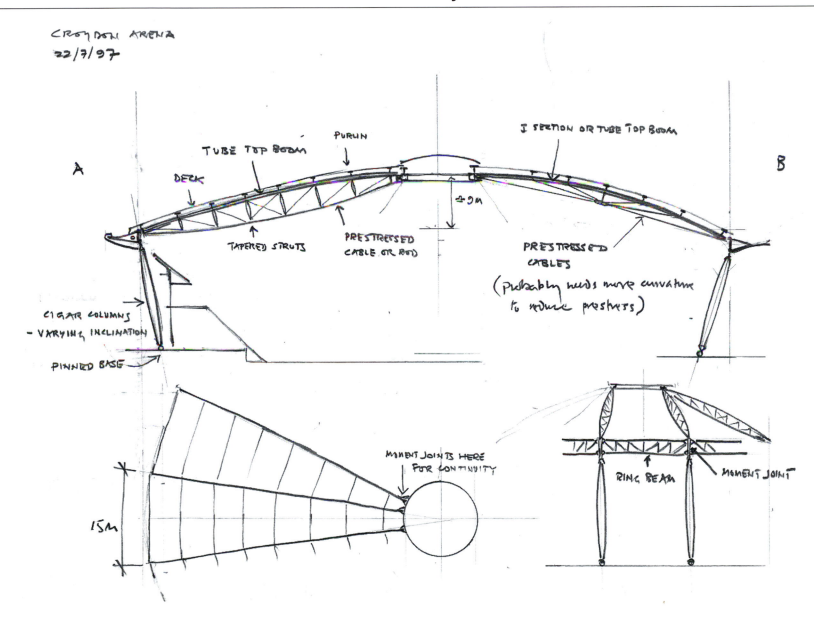

CROYDON ARENA
22/7/97

A

B

J SECTION OR TUBE TOP BOOM

TUBE TOP BOOM

PURLIN

DECK

± 9m

TAPERED STRUTS

PRESTRESSED
CABLE (OR ROD)

PRESTRESSED
CABLES

(Probably needs more curvature
to reduce prestress)

CIGAR COLUMNS
- VARYING INCLINATION

PINNED BASE

15M

MOMENT JOINTS HERE
FOR CONTINUITY

RING BEAM

MOMENT JOINT

CROYDON ARENA
22/7/97

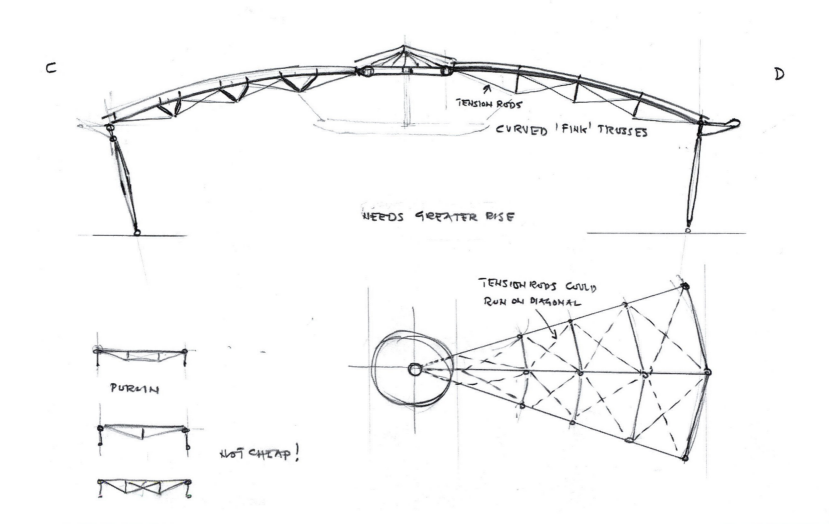

C

D

TENSION RODS

CURVED 'FINK' TRUSSES

NEEDS GREATER RISE

TENSION RODS COULD
RUN ON DIAGONAL

PURLIN

NOT CHEAP!

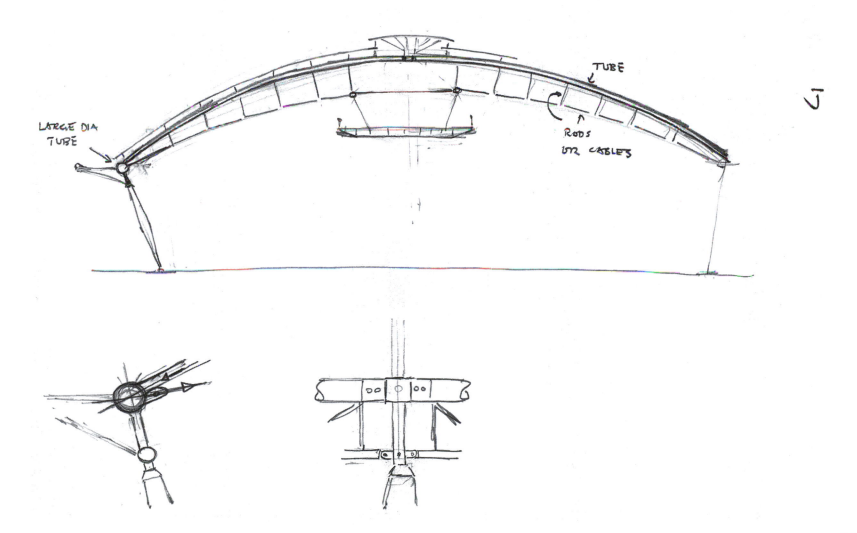

CROYDON ARENA
23/7/97 .

LARGE DIA
TUBE

TUBE

RODS
OR CABLES

Hauptbahnhof

Job: Stuttgart 21, Hauptbahnhof

Client: Deutchbahn

Architect: Wörner + Partner

Date: 1997 – Competition, 2nd prize

- Brief – clear span roof 90m+ span, 400m long as part of major reconstruction of main station for high speed ICE trains
- Part of roof must open for summer air venting – sliding roof proposed
- Earlier conventional truss system by others rejected
- Challenge to design a lighter more elegant structure
- Developed pre-stressed twin tubular arch solution where all members except arches are in tension
- Lateral stability solved in an elegant way

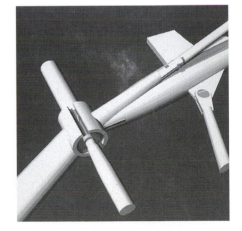

Stuttgart 21
23 . 04 . 97 .

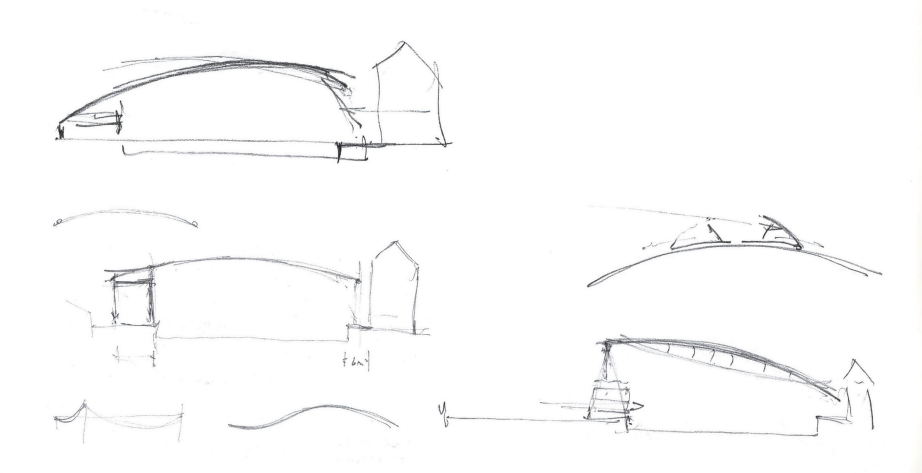

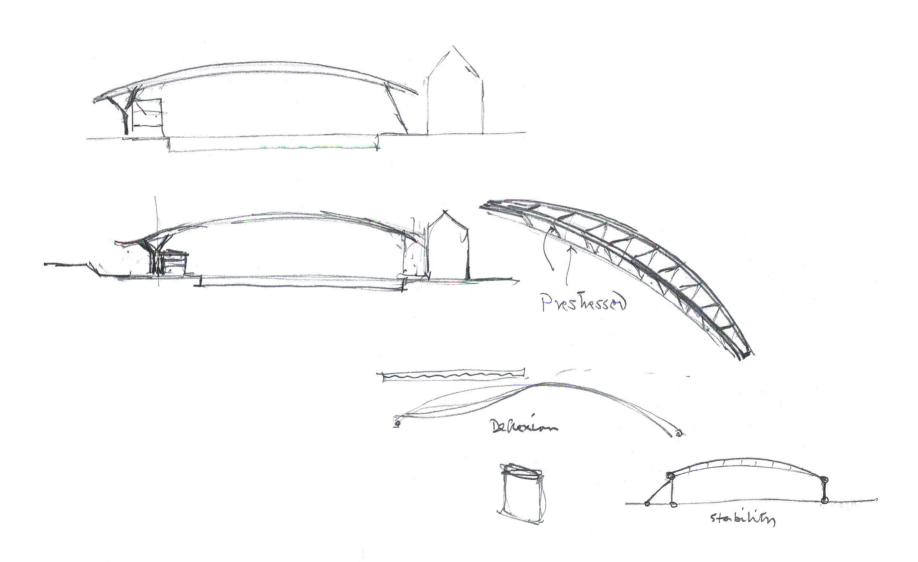

Prestressed

Deflexion

Stability

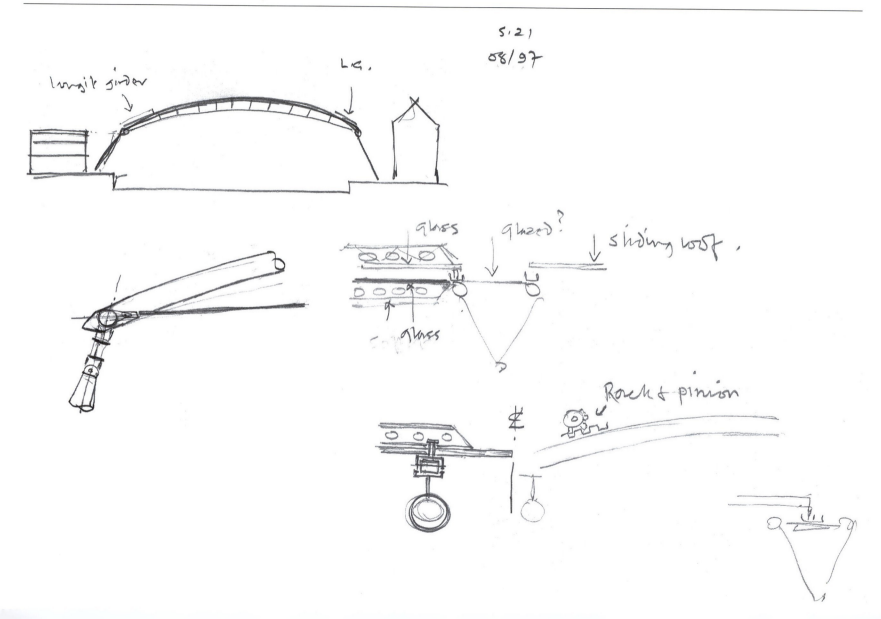

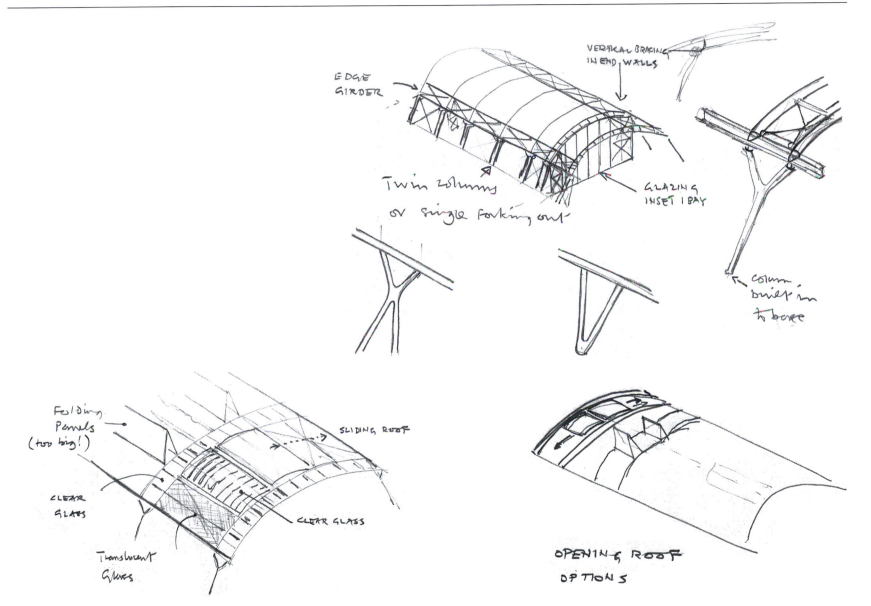

EDGE GIRDER

VERTICAL BRACING
IN END WALLS

GLAZING
INSET 1 BAY

Column
brief into
base

Twin columns
or single forking out

Folding
Panels
(too big!)

SLIDING ROOF

CLEAR
GLASS

CLEAR GLASS

Translucent
Glass

OPENING ROOF
OPTIONS

Stuttgart 21, Hauptbahnhof

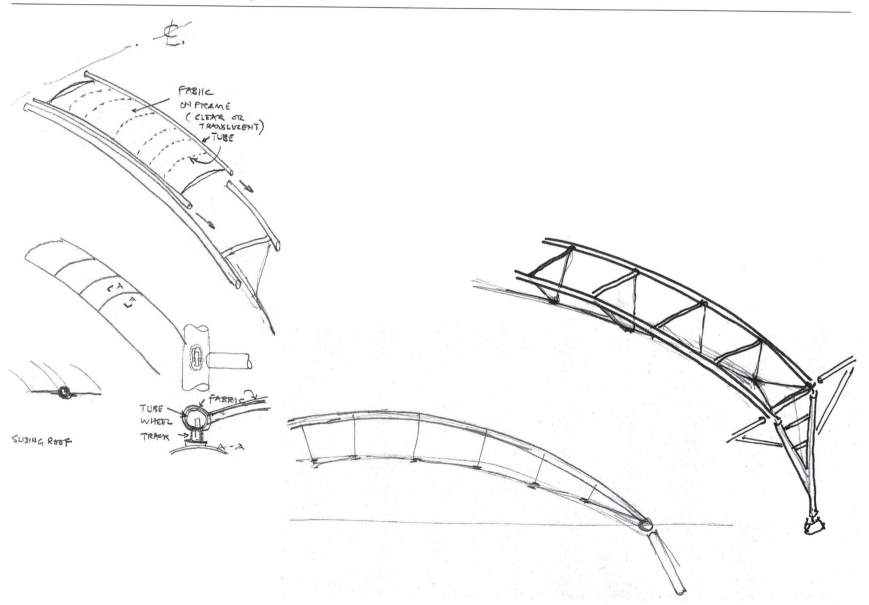

FABRIC
ON FRAME
(CLEAR OR
TRANSLUZENT)
TUBE

SLIDING ROOF

TUBE
WHEEL
TRACK

FABRIC

A - A

Liffey Bridge

Job: Liffey Bridge, Dublin

Client: Dublin City

Architect: Keane Murphy Duff

Date: 1997 – Competition

- Brief – a bridge that complements the adjacent Halfpenny Bridge and does not obscure the river skyline
- Difficult abutment conditions
- Shallow rise to allow disabled access
- Simple twin steel arch solution with deck structure hung from arch
- Glass deck lit from beneath

Liffey Bridge, Dublin

LIFFEY BRIDGE 12/97
(Boxing Day!)

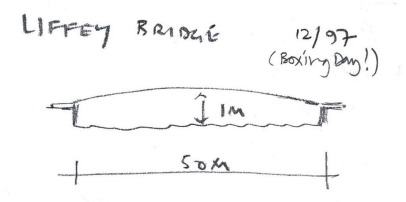

- MAX GRADIENT - 1:20
- SO VERY FLAT BRIDGE REQD.
- SIMPLE FORM NOT TO CONFLICT WITH SURROUNDINGS
- NO MASTS NO CABLES
- SHOULD BE A MODERN METAL STRUCTURE WITH HIGH QUALITY FINISH — LOW MAINTENANCE

- DECK IN ALUMINIUM?
  - RIBBED AS W10.

- DICHROIC LIGHTING IN DECK?

- RIBBED GLASS DECK?

- STRUCTURE:
  1 COMPRESSION ARCH
  2 POST TENSIONED ARCH
  3 MONOCOQUE
  4 POST TENSIONED ARCH (N°2)

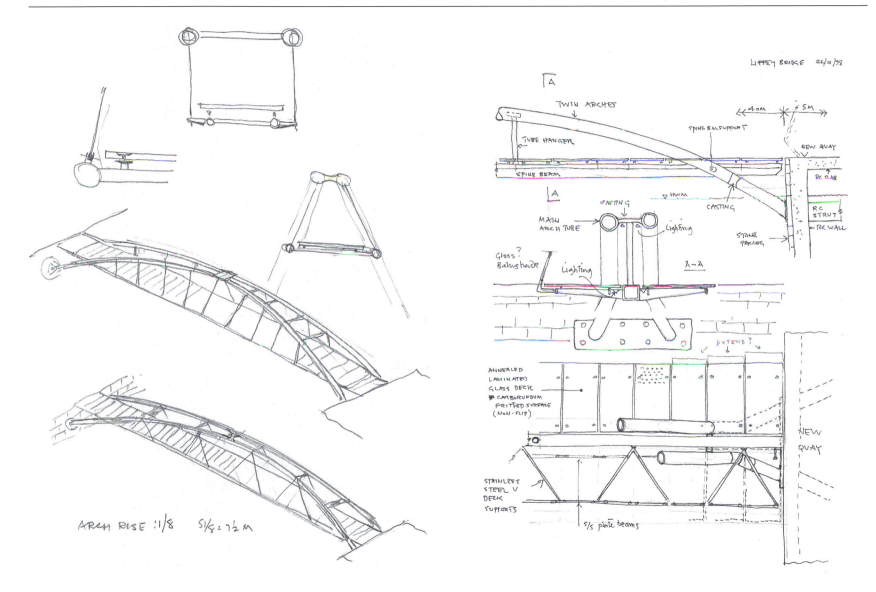

LIFFEY BRIDGE   22/01/98

TWIN ARCHES

TUBE HANGER

SPINE BM. SUPPORT

4·0M   5M

NEW QUAY

SPINE BEAM

RC SLAB

A

CASTING   ▽HWM

RC STRUT

MAIN ARCH TUBE

CASTING

Lighting

RC WALL

Glass? Balustrade

STONE FACING

Lighting

A - A

EXTEND?

ANNEALED LAMINATED GLASS DECK

CARBORUNDUM FRITTED SURFACE (NON-SLIP)

NEW QUAY

STAINLESS STEEL V DECK SUPPORTS

S/S plate beams

ARCH RISE :1/8   S1/8 = 7½ M

Liffey Bridge, Dublin

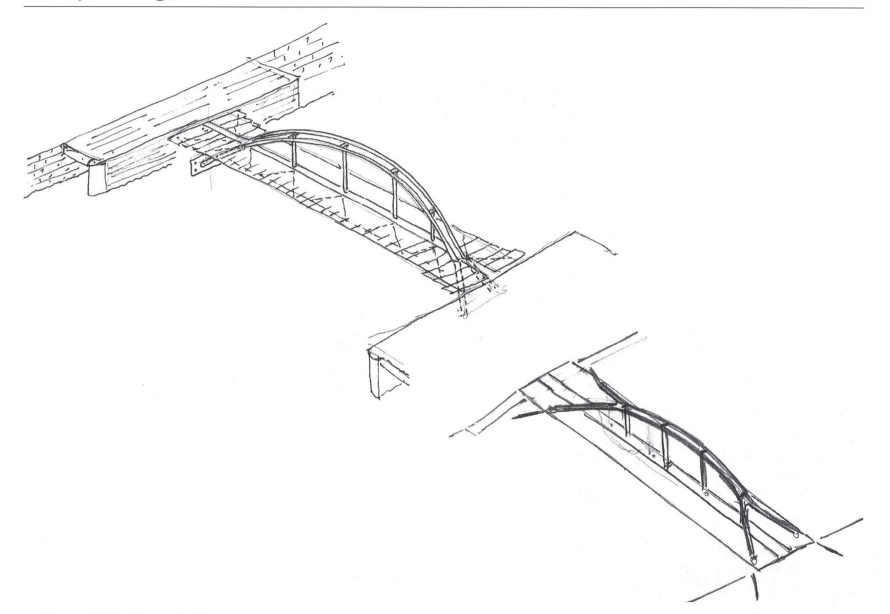

Downing College Boathouse

Job: Downing College Boathouse,
            Cambridge

Client: Downing College, Cambridge

Architect: The Architects Collaborative

Date: 1998 – Project

- A proposal to replace the current unsatisfactory boathouse with a new building
- Site access extremely difficult
- Proposal is to produce a simple elegant 'kit of parts' building with all the above-ground elements brought in by barge
- Simple repetitive steel frame
- Timber panel infill
- Profile metal floor and roof decks

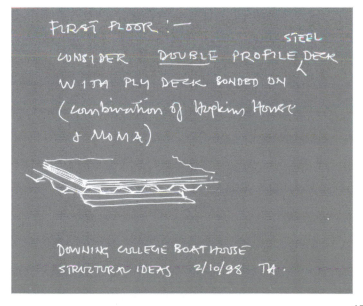

FIRST FLOOR :—
CONSIDER DOUBLE PROFILE DECK STEEL
WITH PLY DECK BONDED ON
(combination of Hopkins House
& MOMA)

DOWNING COLLEGE BOATHOUSE
STRUCTURAL IDEAS   2/10/98 TH.

Downing College Boathouse, Cambridge

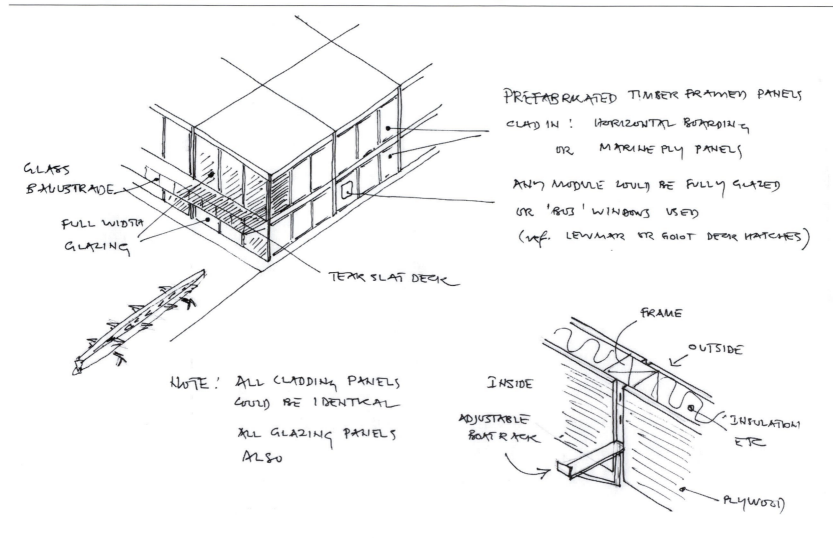

PREFABRICATED TIMBER FRAMED PANELS

CLAD IN : HORIZONTAL BOARDING

OR MARINE PLY PANELS

ANY MODULE COULD BE FULLY GLAZED

OR 'BUS' WINDOWS USED

(ref. LEWMAR OR GOIOT DECK HATCHES)

GLASS BALUSTRADE

FULL WIDTH GLAZING

TEAK SLAT DECK

NOTE : ALL CLADDING PANELS COULD BE IDENTICAL

ALL GLAZING PANELS ALSO

FRAME

OUTSIDE

INSIDE

ADJUSTABLE BOAT RACK

INSULATION ETC

PLYWOOD

DOWNING COLLEGE BOAT HOUSE
CLADDING IDEAS   2/10/98   TA .

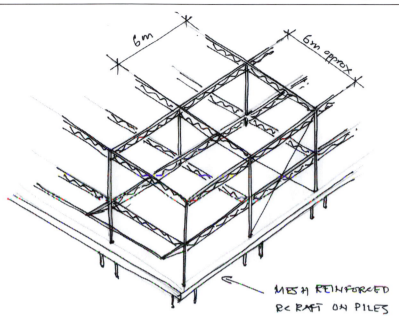

6m

6m approx

MESH REINFORCED
RC RAFT ON PILES

PROFILE METAL OR TIMBER DECK

STRESSED SKIN TIMBER DECK

ROOF LATTICES - SAY 300mm DEEP

FLOOR LATTICES - SAY 450mm DEEP

COLUMNS - SAY 150mm □

WELD OR BOLT BEAM / COL CONNECTIONS

LATTICE BEAM SOLUTION
- GOOD COL/BEAM RIGIDITY
- FAST TO ERECT

ALTERNATIVE!
USE 'MASONITE' TIMBER BEAMS

OR CELLFORM (STEEL)

3 BRACED BAYS

FIRST FLOOR :—
CONSIDER DOUBLE PROFILE STEEL DECK
WITH PLY DECK BONDED ON
(combination of Hopkins House
& MoMA)

DOWNING COLLEGE BOATHOUSE
STRUCTURAL IDEAS 2/10/98 TH.

153

Millennium Pavilion

Preston Candover

Job: Millennium Pavilion, Preston
Candover

Client: Lord Sainsbury of Preston
Candover

Architect: Robert Adam

Date: 1998 – Built

- The brief was for a 'folly' whereby the dome would appear to float above the supporting stone column structure
- The copper-clad dome shell is a cast aluminium diagrid supported on a stainless steel plate ring beam
- The ring beam is supported on slender tube columns braced by cold drawn rods also in stainless steel

Note: At sunset the dome really does appear to float

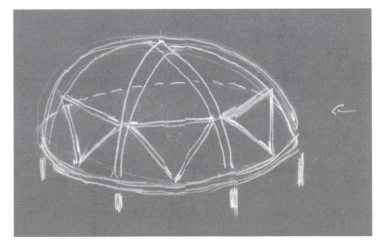

Millennium Pavilion, Preston Candover

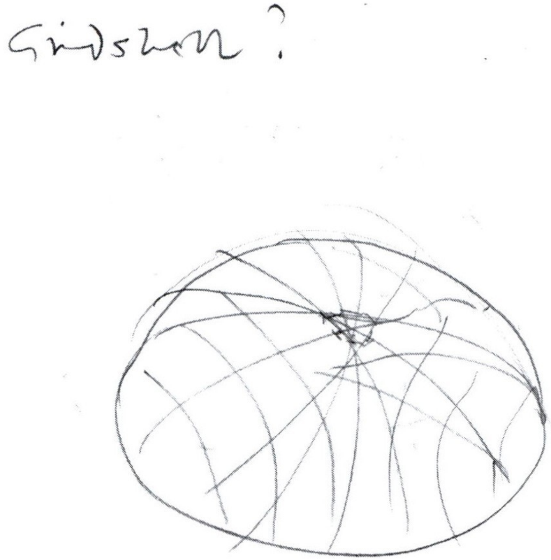

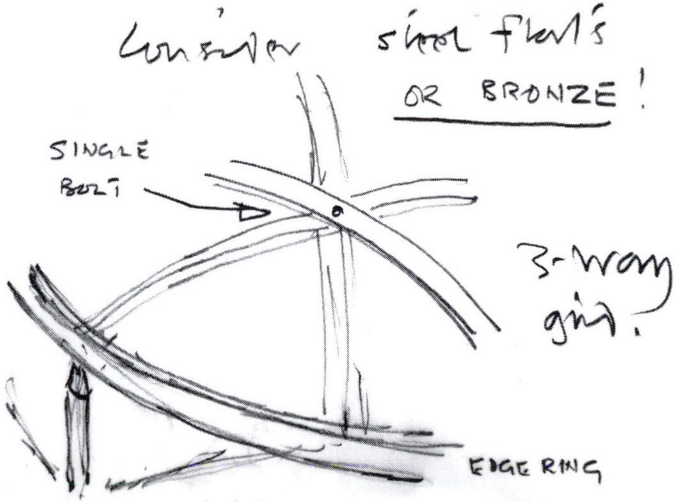

Gridshell ?

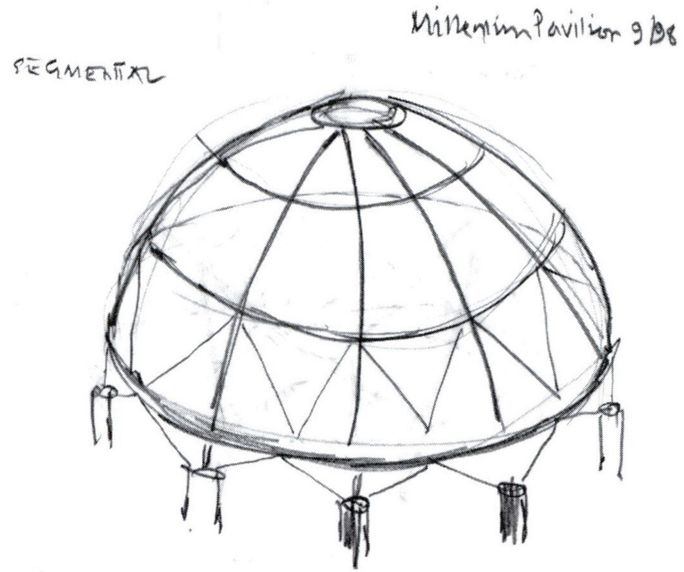

SEGMENTAL

Millennium Pavilion 9/98

Consider steel flat's
OR BRONZE!

SINGLE BOLT

3-way grid.

EDGE RING

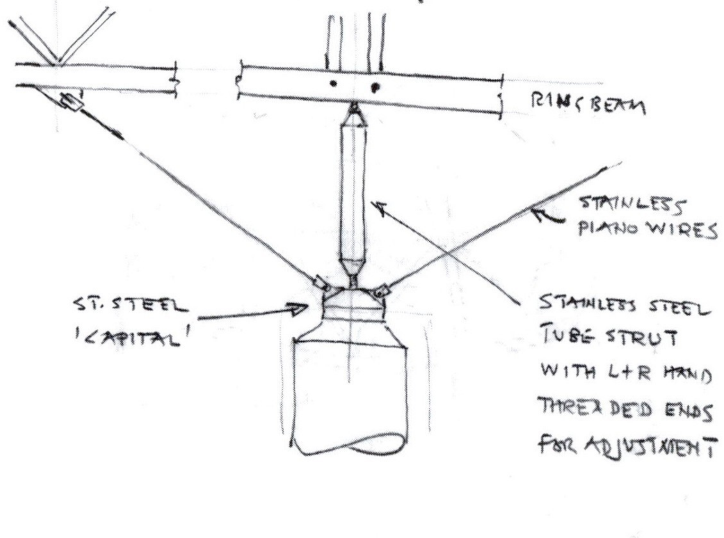

RING BEAM

ST. STEEL 'CAPITAL'

STAINLESS PIANO WIRES

STAINLESS STEEL TUBE STRUT WITH L+R HAND THREADED ENDS FOR ADJUSTMENT

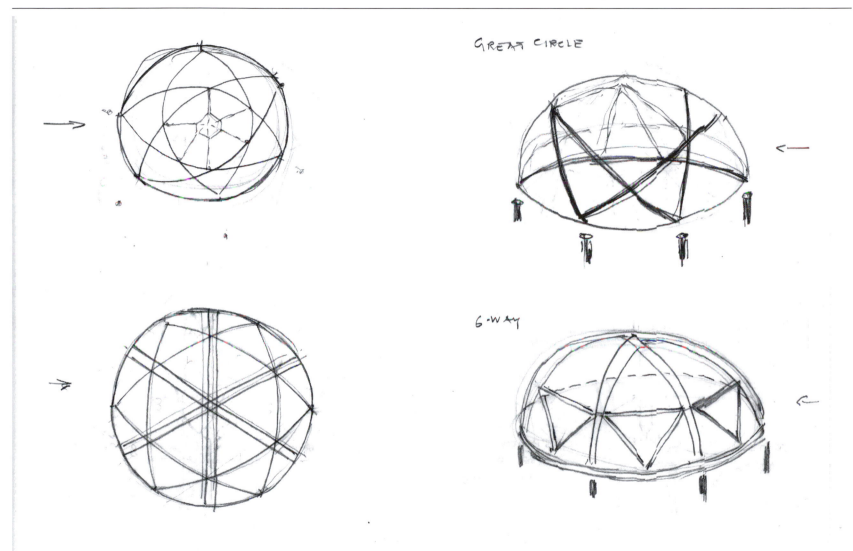

GREAT CIRCLE

6-WAY

Millennium Pavilion, Preston Candover

BASIC CONSTRUCTION
TECHNIQUE

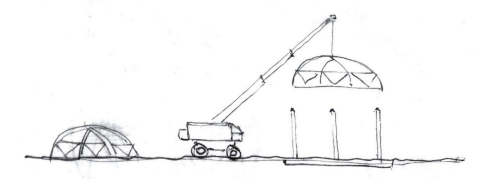

ASSEMBLE DOME
ON GROUND FROM
PRE FORMED & FINISHED
PARTS

CAST FOUNDATIONS
FIX COLUMNS IN PLACE
AS VERTICAL CANTILEVERS

LIFT COMPLETE DOME INTO PLACE

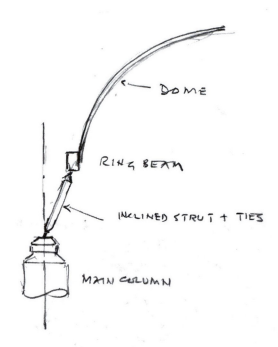

DOME

RING BEAM

INCLINED STRUT + TIES

MAIN COLUMN

DOME SET INSIDE COLUMN CIRCLE

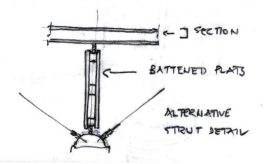

J SECTION

BATTENED PLATS

ALTERNATIVE
STRUT DETAIL

Materials for framework

Stainless steel (matt finish) poss.

Bronze   no

Aluminium   yes

Timber   – no

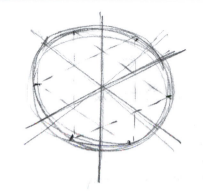

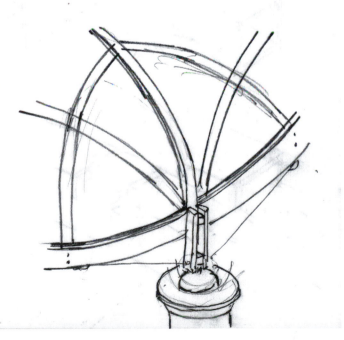

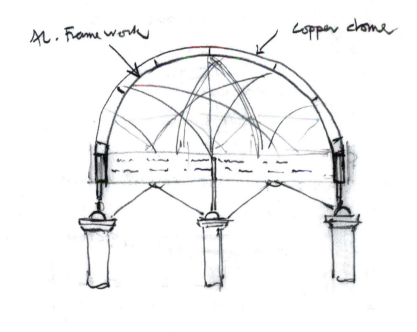

Al. Framework   Copper dome

AWA Sewage Treatment Plant

Lowestoft

Job: AWA Sewage Treatment Plant,
Lowestoft

Client: Anglian Water Authority/Mowlem

Architect: Barber Casanovers and Ruffles

Date: 1998 – In design

- Low profile building on a
  sensitive site
- Structural options for very large
  elliptical enclosure
- Clear span air supported as an idea
- Internal columns more sensible
  and economic
- Design for maximum repetition of
  common structural elements
- Great opportunity to explore a
  range of ideas for covering a large
  industrial space
- Possible prototype for future sites to
  conform to EC regulations

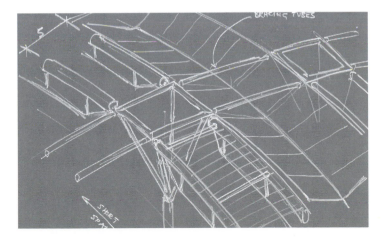

AWA Sewage Treatment Plant, Lowestoft

AWA Lowestoft   15/07/99

AWA Lowestoft   15/07/99

Alternative Roof Cladding Types

- Profile metal — deep or shallow with purlins

- Fabric — PVDF / polyester   15/20 yr life
  Teflon / glass   25 yr life.

- Foil — ETFE

OR   totally air supported.

Column Grid

Say 20 x 20 M

Max col. Height — 15 M

AIR-SUPPORTED STRUCTURE
WITH 'TREES' AS TIE-DOWNS
AND SUPPORTS IN THE EVENT OF PRESSURE
FAILURE — ENERGY IN USE? METHANE

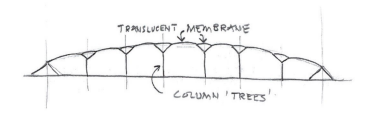

TRANSLUCENT MEMBRANE

COLUMN 'TREES'

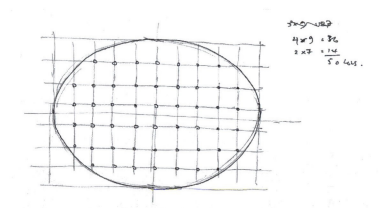

3x9 =27
4x9 = 36
2x7 = 14
———
50 cols.

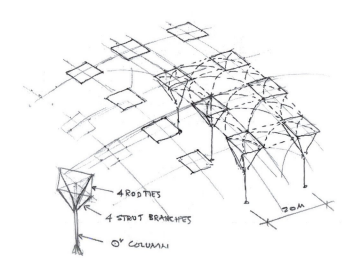

4 ROD TIES

4 STRUT BRANCHES

O" COLUMN

20M

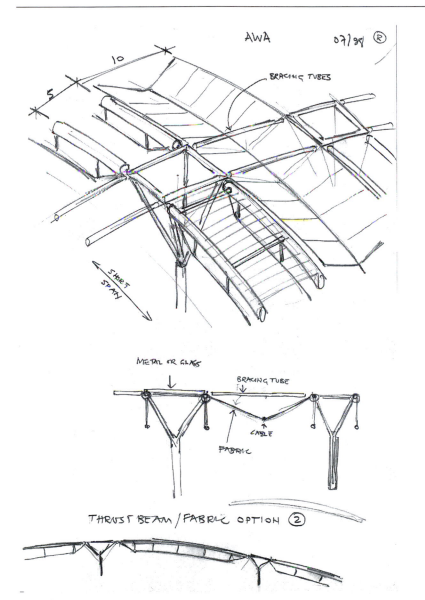

AWA   07/98 ®

10

5

BRACING TUBES

SHORT SPAN

METAL OR GLASS

BRACING TUBE

CABLE

FABRIC

THRUST BEAM / FABRIC OPTION ②

AWA Lowestoft 7/98

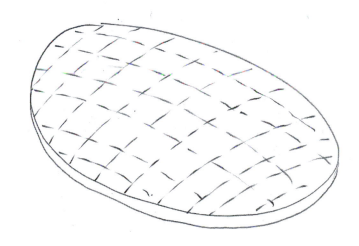

FABRIC / 2-WAY CABLE
AIR SUPPORTED STRUCTURE

AWA Sewage Treatment Plant, Lowestoft

AWA Lowestoft 7/98 (R)

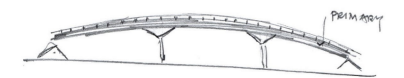

PRIMARY

CROSS SECTION.

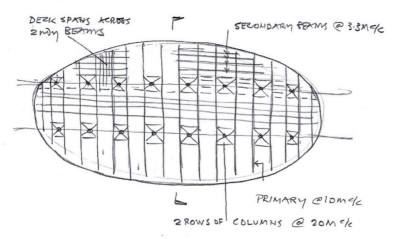

DECK SPANS ACROSS 2ndRY BEAMS

SECONDARY BEAMS @ 3.3M c/c

PRIMARY @ 10M c/c

2 ROWS OF COLUMNS @ 20M c/c

SAVES ON COLUMNS + FOUNDATIONS

STEEL/ALUMINIUM ROOF OPTION ②

Canary Wharf Bridge

London Docklands

Job: Canary Wharf Bridge, London
Docklands

Client: London Docklands Development
Corporation

Architect: Eva Jiricna

Date: 1999 – Competition entry

- A bridge at high level to link an
  existing building with a proposed
  new building
- Tubular steel lattice girders span
  between buildings
- Cladding is glass to both sides and
  the roof, with ventilation slots in the
  floor

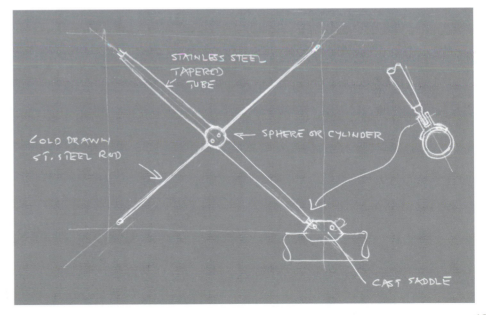

Canary Wharf Bridge, London Docklands

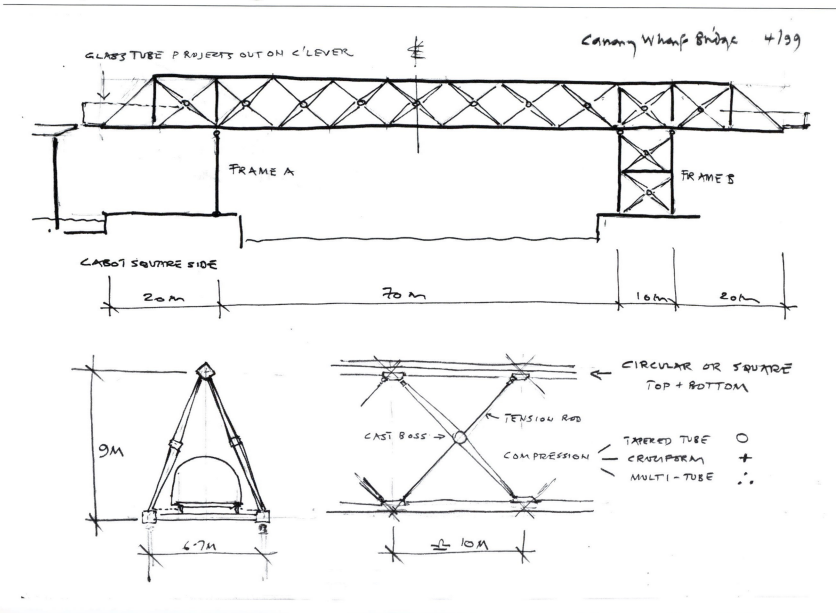

GLASS TUBE PROJECTS OUT ON C'LEVER

Canary Wharf Bridge   4/99

FRAME A

FRAME B

CABOT SQUARE SIDE

20M   70M   16M   20M

9M

6·7M

CIRCULAR OR SQUARE
TOP + BOTTOM

TENSION ROD

CAST BOSS →

COMPRESSION

TAPERED TUBE   O

CRUCIFORM   +

MULTI-TUBE   ∴

10M

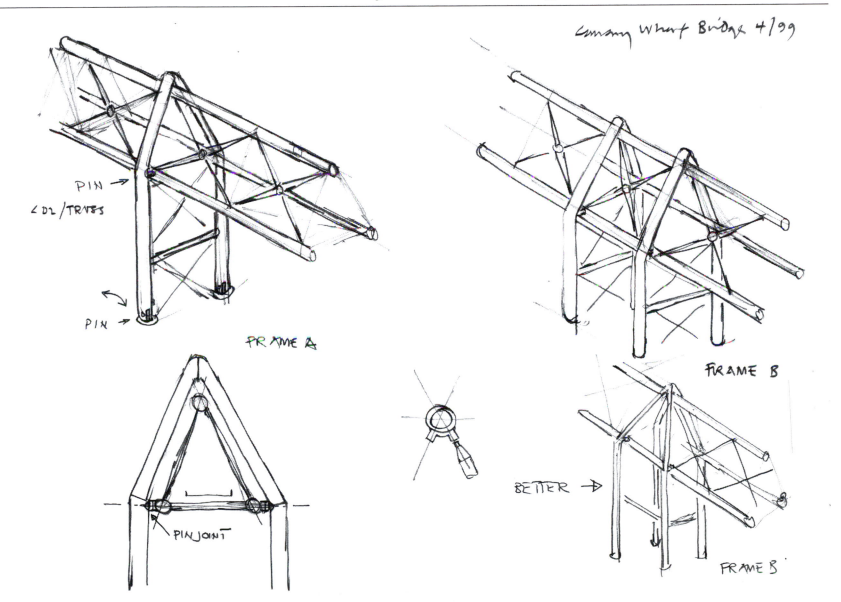

Canary Wharf Bridge 4/99

PIN

∠D2/TRUSS

PIN

FRAME A

PIN JOINT

FRAME B

BETTER →

FRAME B

Canary Wharf Bridge, London Docklands

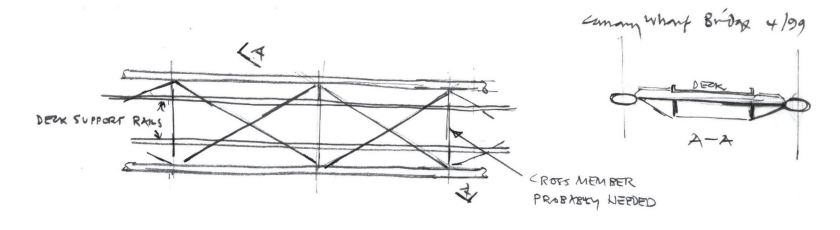

Canary Wharf Bridge 4/99

DECK

A—A

DECK SUPPORT RAILS

CROSS MEMBER PROBABLY NEEDED

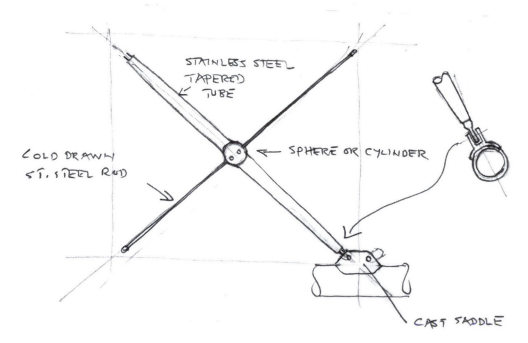

STAINLESS STEEL TAPERED TUBE

COLD DRAWN ST. STEEL ROD

SPHERE OR CYLINDER

CAST SADDLE

Florida Canopies

Job: Florida Canopies, Florida

Client: Florida Southern College

Architect: John McAslan and Partners

Date: 2000 – Project

- The original canopies, in reinforced concrete, were designed by Frank Lloyd Wright
- Many needed replacing due to corrosion and the canopy system extended
- The form of the proposed new canopies was designed to be in sympathy with the original with triangular and faceted forms but in aluminium rather than concrete
- Designed as a repetitive modular system which could be stepped to cope with level differences

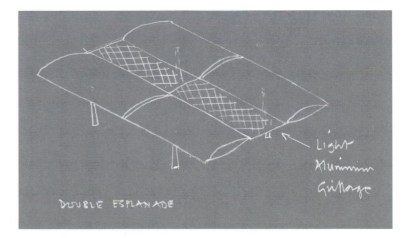

DOUBLE ESPLANADE

Light Aluminium Grillage

Florida Southern College Apr '99

Replacement of F.L. Wright canopies

Climate : Hot + Humid

Materials : Corrosion Resistant-

GRP, Aluminium, CarbonFibre?

IDEAS : Modular, Kit System, Sandwich panel

1 Column type

1 or 2 roof types

FORM

X ?   X

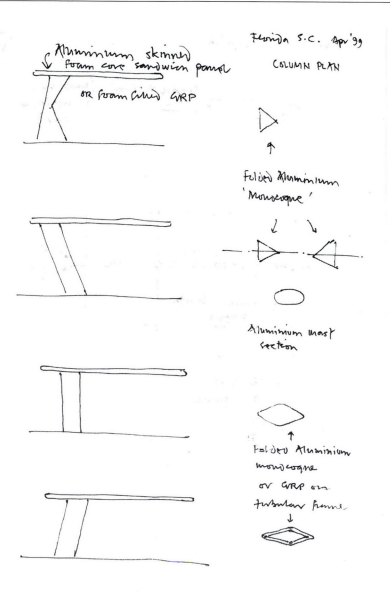

Aluminium skinned
foam core sandwich panel
or foam filled GRP

Florida S.C. Apr '99
COLUMN PLAN

Folded Aluminium
'Monocoque'

Aluminium mast
section

Folded Aluminium
monocoque
or GRP on
tubular frame

Florida S.C. Apv '99

Florida S.C. 31/8/99

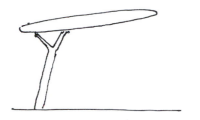

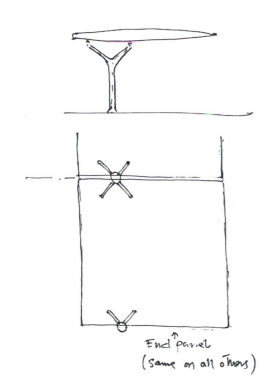

End panel
(same on all others)

Queries

- Are existing FLW Esplenades to be replaced?

- Campus IT — in canopy structure
  OR Below ground

- Stepping of units —

  A Single discrete units

  B Double units

- Is the ground stepped or sloping (photos show slips)

- The existing column grid appears to be about 14ft.

- ✳ Wind tunnel testing required (Hurricanes)

- 'Airfoil' designed for ZERO lift.

Florida Canopies, Florida, USA

Florida SC 8/99

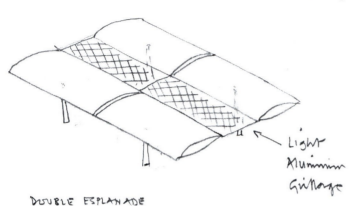

DOUBLE ESPLANADE

Light Aluminium Grillage

• CLADDING TO COLUMNS —

'RIGIDIZED' ALUMINIUM PLATE

EXTRUDED ALUMINIUM 'DECK'

• JUNCTION BETWEEN PANELS

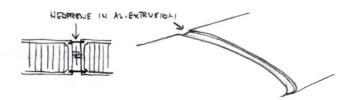

NEOPRENE IN AL.EXTRUSION

Kelvin Link Bridge

Glasgow

Job: Kelvin Link Bridge, Glasgow

Client: University of Glasgow

Architect: John McAslan and Partners

Date: Current

- The winner of a competition to form a pedestrian link from the University to the Art Gallery across the river Kelvin gorge
- Tubular steel asymmetric trestles on the banks of the river support a curved tubular steel beam with steel outriggers
- A pair of arches, inclined towards one another, span the centre section
- The concrete deck is supported on the outriggers
- A secondary bridge, forming a route to give access to the river bank, is cantilevered from the main bridge

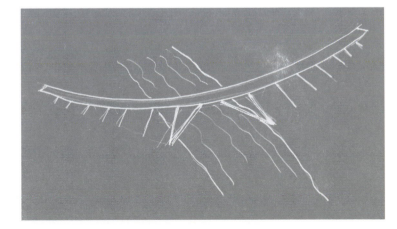

Kelvin Link Bridge, Glasgow

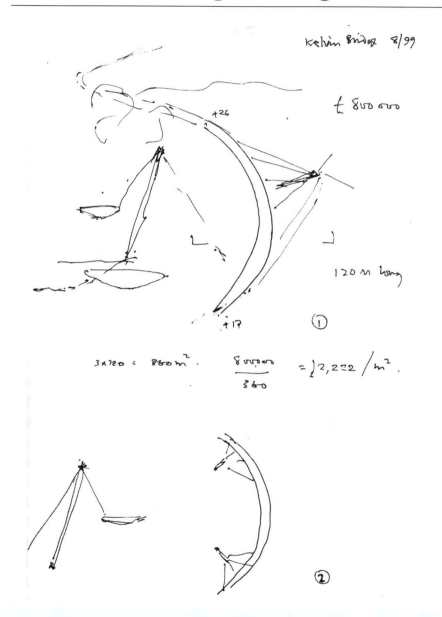

Kelvin Bridge 8/99

£ 800 000

+26

120 m long

+17

①

3 × 120 = 860 m² $\frac{800000}{360}$ = £2,222 / m² .

②

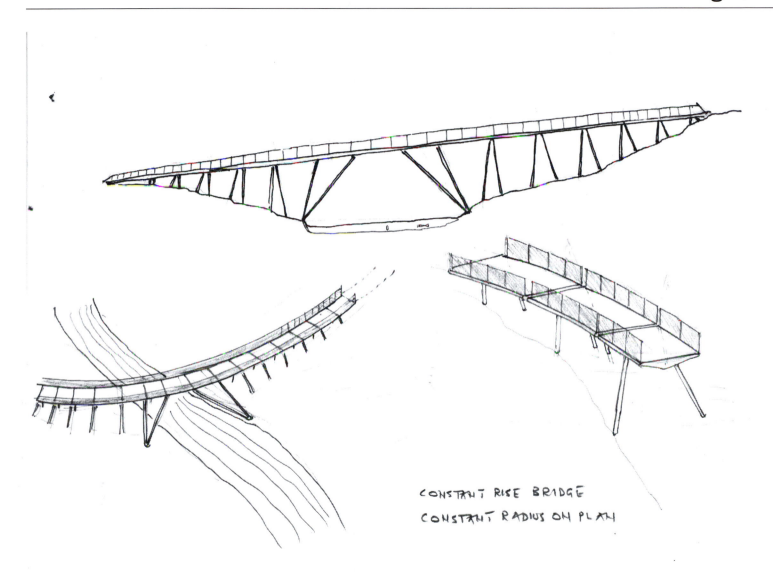

CONSTANT RISE BRIDGE
CONSTANT RADIUS ON PLAN

Kelvin Bridge 8/90

Kelvin Link Bridge, Glasgow

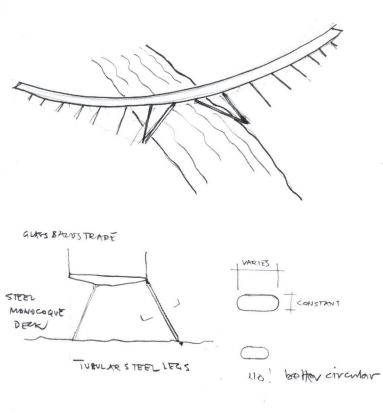

Kelvin Bridge 8/99

GLASS BALUSTRADE

STEEL
MONOCOQUE
DECK

TUBULAR STEEL LEGS

VARIES

CONSTANT

no! better circular

X

Blackfriars Station Renewal

London

Job: Blackfriars Station Renewal, London

Client: Railtrack

Architect: Alsop and Stormer

Date: 2000

- Alternative designs for a new station roof to be built over the existing rail tracks on Blackfriars Bridge
- New loads have to be distributed back to existing bridge piers
- Structure to be as light as possible

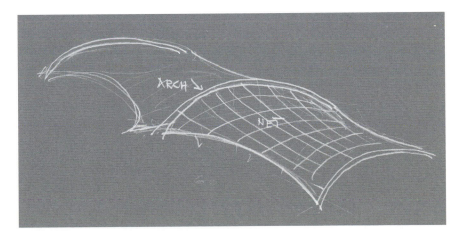

Blackfriars Station Renewal, London

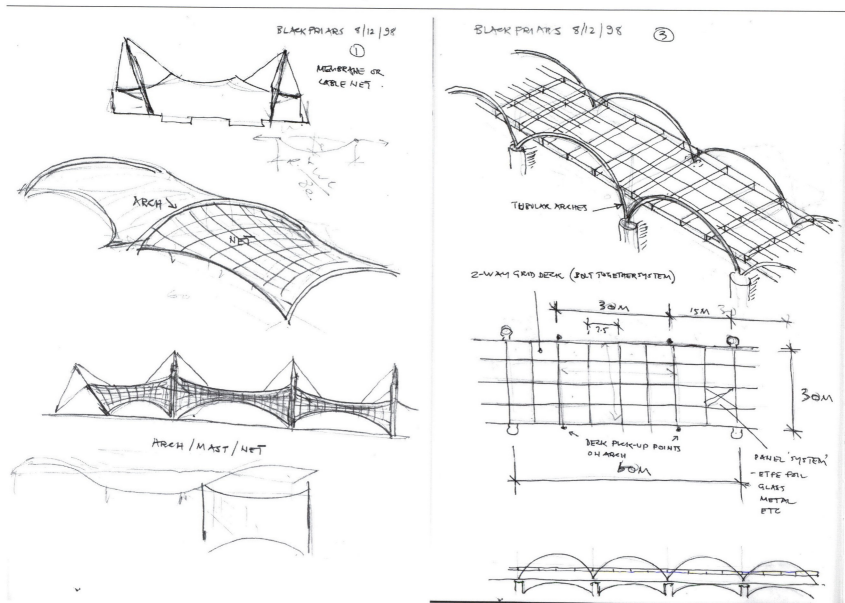

BLACK FRIARS 8/12/98 ①

MEMBRANE OR CABLE NET.

ARCH ↓

NET

ARCH / MAST / NET

BLACK FRIARS 8/12/98 ③

TUBULAR ARCHES

2-WAY GRID DECK (BOLT TOGETHER SYSTEM)

3@M   15M

7.5

30M

DECK PICK-UP POINTS ON ARCH

60M

PANEL 'SYSTEM'
- ETFE FOIL
GLASS
METAL
ETC

Royal Albert Bridge

Saltash

Job: Royal Albert Bridge, Saltash

Designer: Isambard Kingdom Brunel

Date: 1859 – Built

Exhibition: 2000

- The Design Museum asked me to carry out a largely diagrammatic analysis of Brunel's bridge for an exhibition of his work
- The drawings and text explain its extraordinarily advanced structural concept and compare it with his earlier design for the Clifton suspension bridge over the Avon Gorge in Bristol

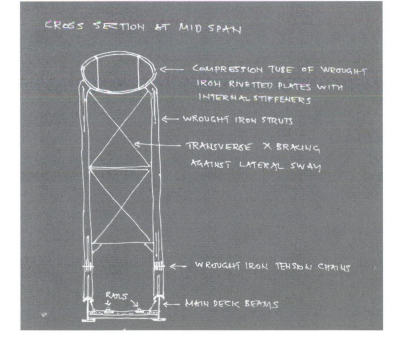

CROSS SECTION AT MID SPAN

← COMPRESSION TUBE OF WROUGHT IRON RIVETTED PLATES WITH INTERNAL STIFFENERS

← WROUGHT IRON STRUTS

← TRANSVERSE X BRACING AGAINST LATERAL SWAY

← WROUGHT IRON TENSION CHAINS

RAILS

← MAIN DECK BEAMS

I K BRUNEL — SALTASH BRIDGE

BUILT BETWEEN 1853 and 1859

"WHY IS SALTASH BRIDGE BRUNEL'S MASTERPIECE

OR IS CLIFTON SUSPENSION BRIDGE BETTER"

— QUESTION FROM PAUL THOMPSON, DESIGN MUSEUM

DIRECTOR TO TONY HUNT   MAR 2000

CLIFTON SUSPENSION BRIDGE IS JUST THAT — A

SUSPENSION BRIDGE WITH WROUGHT IRON TENSION

CHAINS & HANGERS SUPPORTED ON STONE ARCHES.

ITS SETTING HIGH ACROSS THE AVON GORGE IS

SPECTACULAR :—

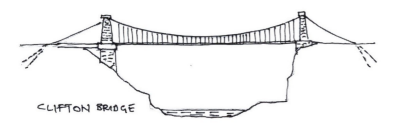

CLIFTON BRIDGE

BUT SALTASH IS UNIQUE IN ITS DESIGN AND

FORM OF CONSTRUCTION

SALTASH IS A COMBINATION OF 3 CLASSICAL ENGINEERING

FORMS :—

    THE COMPRESSION ARCH

    THE TENSION CHAINS

    THE BEAM DECK

THE PRINCIPLE   — A BOWSTRING

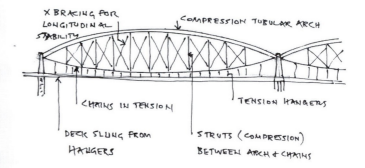

X BRACING FOR LONGITUDINAL STABILITY

COMPRESSION TUBULAR ARCH

CHAINS IN TENSION

TENSION HANGERS

DECK SLUNG FROM HANGERS

STRUTS (COMPRESSION) BETWEEN ARCH & CHAINS

THE OUTWARD THRUST OF THE ARCH IS

COUNTERACTED BY THE TENSION CHAINS

WITH THE STRUTS HOLDING THE TWO

ELEMENTS APART

←SUPPORT

■— MEMBERS IN COMPRESSION   ←→

— MEMBERS IN TENSION   →←

THE COMPRESSION TUBE

THE TUBE IS OVAL IN CROSS-SECTION

THIS SHAPE PROVIDES EXTRA LATERAL (SIDEWAYS) STIFFNESS FOR WIND LOADS AND ALLOWS SMOOTHER WIND FLOW

CROSS SECTION AT MID SPAN

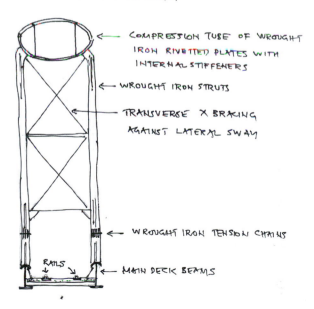

← COMPRESSION TUBE OF WROUGHT IRON RIVETTED PLATES WITH INTERNAL STIFFENERS

← WROUGHT IRON STRUTS

← TRANSVERSE X BRACING AGAINST LATERAL SWAY

← WROUGHT IRON TENSION CHAINS

← MAIN DECK BEAMS

PREFABRICATION

THE MAIN SPANS EACH 455 FT (138·7 M.) LONG WERE FULLY PREFABRICATED ON THE SHORE FLOATED IN THE RIVER ON PONTOONS AND THEN PROGRESSIVELY JACKED UP THE PIERS TO THEIR FINAL POSITION 100 FT (30·5 M) ABOVE THE RIVER LEVEL.

EACH COMPLETE SPAN WEIGHED IN EXCESS OF 1500 TONS.

THE FOUNDATION + PIER STUDY IS A SEPARATE STORY

SALTASH IS IN EFFECT A SUSPENSION BRIDGE — THE DECK IS HUNG FROM CHAINS.

IT IS A RARE TYPE USING WHAT IS CALLED A 'CLOSED SYSTEM' IE THE FORCES ARE ALL CONTAINED WITHIN THE STRUCTURE

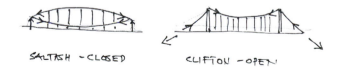

SALTASH - CLOSED   CLIFTON - OPEN

CERTAINLY IN TERMS OF RAILWAY BRIDGES SALTASH IS UNIQUE - AND VERY CLEVER

TH 6/00

'Ballet' Bridge, Covent Garden

Job: 'Ballet' Bridge, Covent Garden, London

Client: Royal Opera House

Architect: Jeremy Dixon, Edward Jones

Date: 2001 – Competition

- A bridge at high level linking the Royal Opera House to the new Ballet School hence the name chosen by the architects
- A semi-monocoque steel deck supporting cruciform cross-section hoops forming a diamond pattern glazed tube

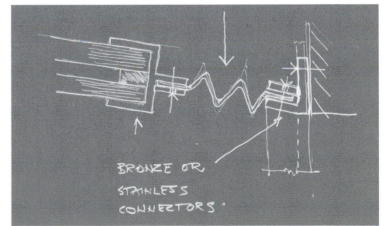

BRONZE OR STAINLESS CONNECTORS

'Ballet' Bridge, Covent Garden, London

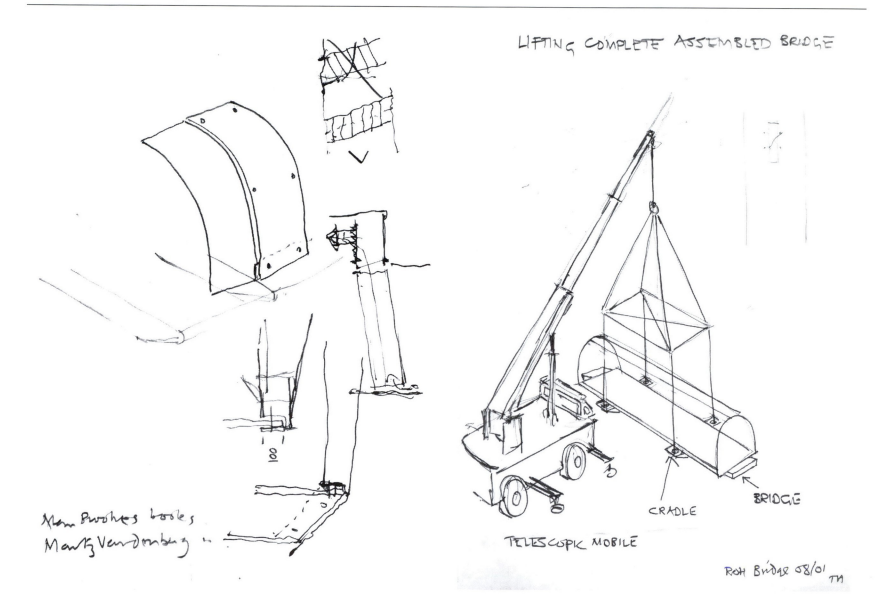

LIFTING COMPLETE ASSEMBLED BRIDGE

TELESCOPIC MOBILE

CRADLE

BRIDGE

Mom Prostes books,
Marty Vandonburg "

ROH Bridge 08/01 TM

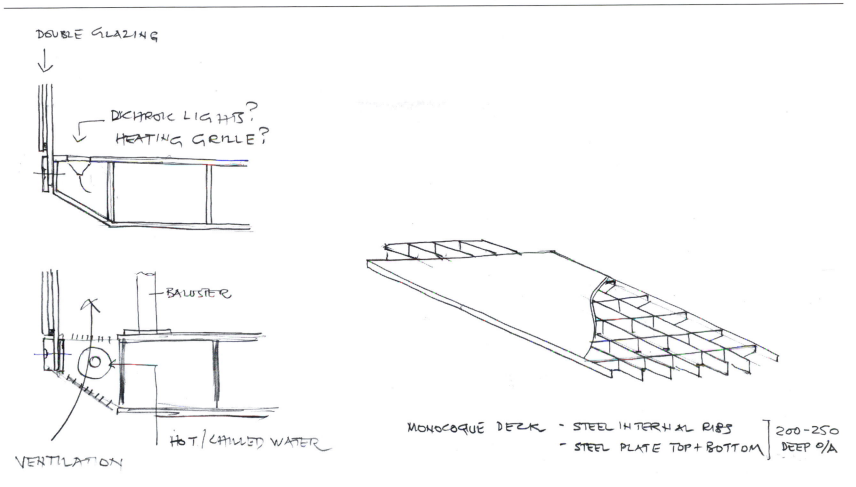

DOUBLE GLAZING

DICHROIC LIGHTS?
HEATING GRILLE?

BALUSTER

VENTILATION

HOT/CHILLED WATER

ROH Bridge 08/01 TA

MONOCOQUE DECK - STEEL INTERNAL RIBS
- STEEL PLATE TOP + BOTTOM] 200-250 DEEP O/A

'Ballet' Bridge, Covent Garden, London

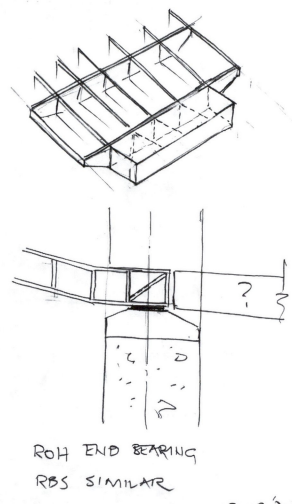

ROH END BEARING

RBS SIMILAR

ROH Bridge 08/01
TA

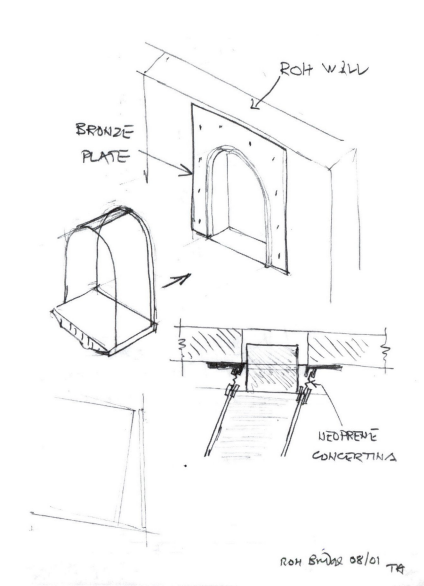

ROH WALL

BRONZE
PLATE

NEOPRENE
CONCERTINA

ROH Bridge 08/01 TA

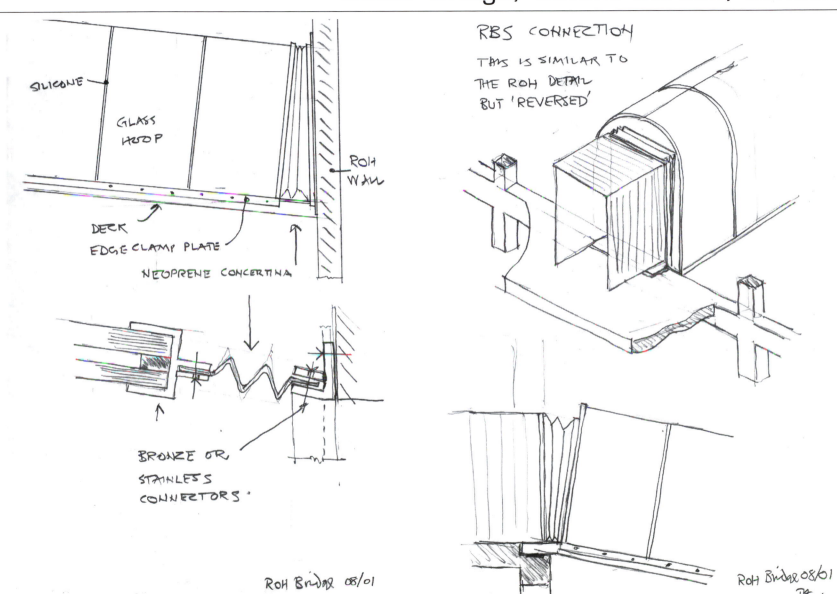

SILICONE

GLASS HOOP

ROH WALL

DECK
EDGE CLAMP PLATE

NEOPRENE CONCERTINA

BRONZE OR STAINLESS CONNECTORS

RBS CONNECTION

THIS IS SIMILAR TO THE ROH DETAIL BUT 'REVERSED'

ROH Bridge 08/01

ROH Bridge 08/01
TA

Empress State Redevelopment

London

Job: Empress State Redevelopment,
London

Client: Land Securities

Architect: Wilkinson Eyre

Date: 2002 – Under construction

- The conversion and extension of a 1900s 27-storey commercial concrete frame building
- One part of the proposal is to extend the south-facing floor plate by 5 metres from level 3 to roof
- The existing columns were not capable of taking extra load and therefore a means had to be found to carry the new loads down to an already close-packed foundation arrangement
- Various ideas were explored of which these sketches illustrate in early form an idea for carrying the new loads down to new foundations.
- The 5 metre slab extension is independent of both the existing columns and the slab edge

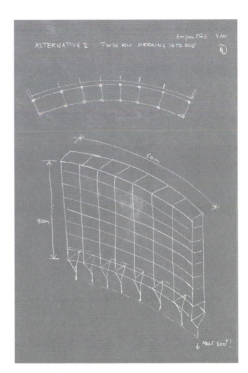

Empress State Redevelopment, London

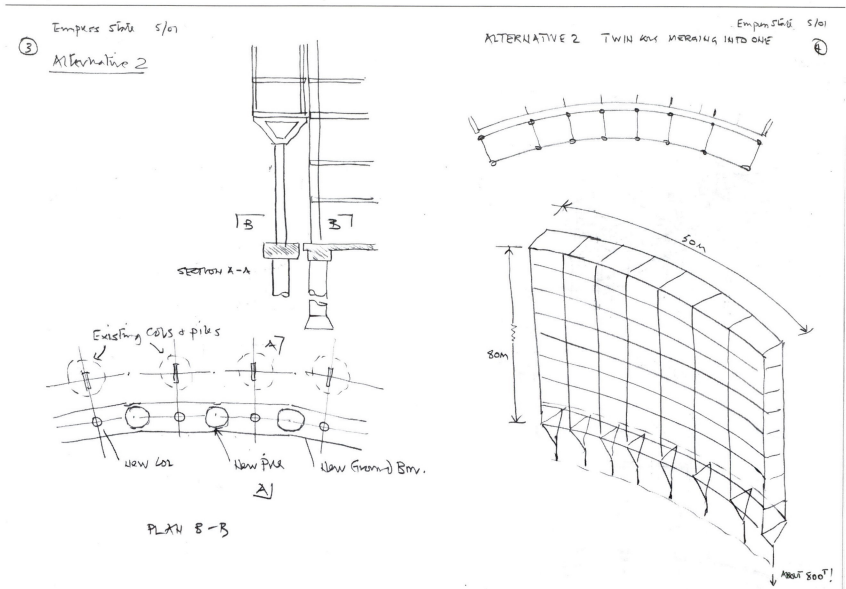

Empress State 5/07

③ Alternative 2

SECTION A-A

B   B

Existing cols & piles

New col   New Pile   New (Ground) Bm.

A

PLAN B-B

Empress State 5/01

ALTERNATIVE 2   TWIN cols MERGING INTO ONE ④

50M

80M

ABOUT 800ᵀ!

Hilcote House Bridge

Job: Hilcote House Bridge, Hilcote

Client: Mr and Mrs Mick Newton

Designer: Tony and Julian Hunt

Date: 2002 – Under construction

- Alternative ideas for an internal bridge linking two buildings at first floor level
- Simpler version chosen, called the 'aerodeck'
- Full monocoque construction considered but abandoned due to difficult site access
- Construction is a combination of steel, timber and glass producing a calm design with minimal impact on the space which it occupies

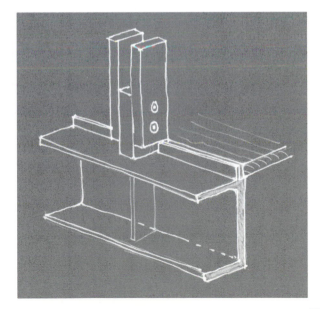

Hilcote House Bridge, Hilcote

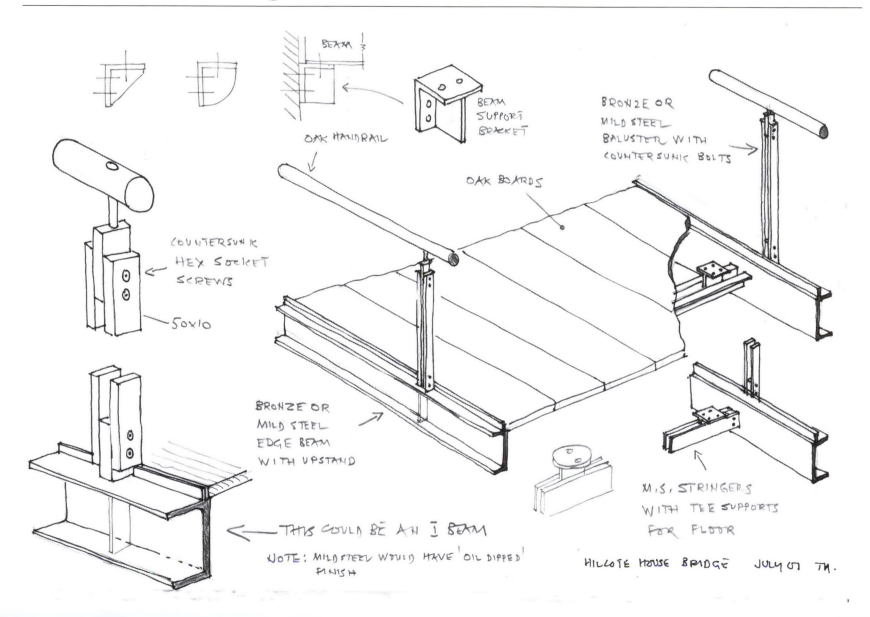

BEAM $\frac{1}{3}$

OAK HANDRAIL

BEAM SUPPORT BRACKET

BRONZE OR MILD STEEL BALUSTER WITH COUNTERSUNK BOLTS

OAK BOARDS

COUNTERSUNK HEX SOCKET SCREWS

50x10

BRONZE OR MILD STEEL EDGE BEAM WITH UPSTAND

M.S. STRINGERS WITH TEE SUPPORTS FOR FLOOR

THIS COULD BE AN I BEAM

NOTE: MILD STEEL WOULD HAVE 'OIL DIPPED' FINISH

HILCOTE HOUSE BRIDGE   JULY 07   TM.

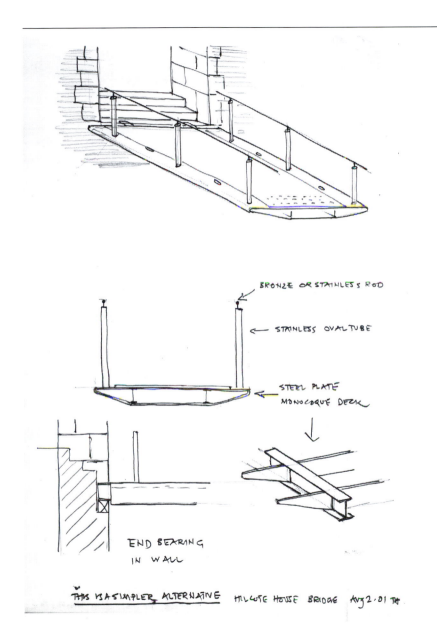

BRONZE OR STAINLESS ROD

← STAINLESS OVAL TUBE

STEEL PLATE
MONOCOQUE DECK

END BEARING
IN WALL

THIS IS A SIMPLER ALTERNATIVE   HILCOTE HOUSE BRIDGE   Aug 2·01 TA

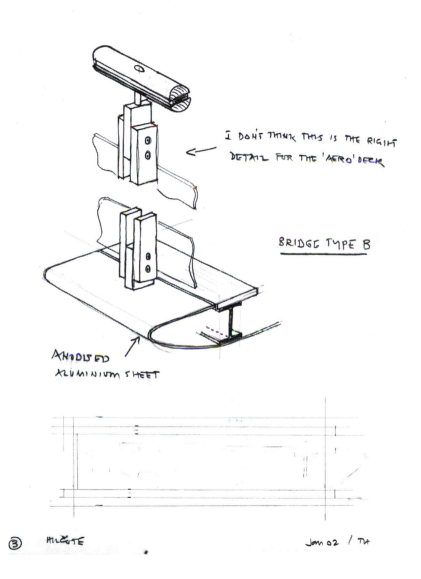

I DON'T THINK THIS IS THE RIGHT
DETAIL FOR THE 'AERO' DECK

BRIDGE TYPE B

ANODISED
ALUMINIUM SHEET

③   HILCOTE   Jan 02 / TA

Hilcote House Bridge, Hilcote

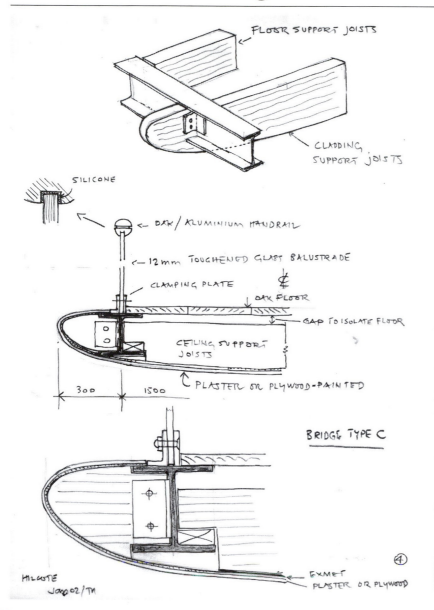

FLOOR SUPPORT JOISTS

CLADDING SUPPORT JOISTS

SILICONE

← OAK / ALUMINIUM HANDRAIL

← 12mm TOUGHENED GLASS BALUSTRADE

CLAMPING PLATE

OAK FLOOR

GAP TO ISOLATE FLOOR

CEILING SUPPORT JOISTS

PLASTER OR PLYWOOD - PAINTED

300   1500

BRIDGE TYPE C

④

EXMET PLASTER OR PLYWOOD

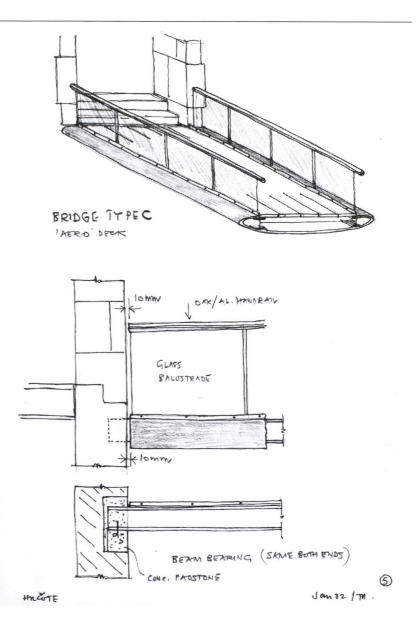

BRIDGE TYPE C
'AERO' DECK

10mm   OAK/AL. HANDRAIL

GLASS BALUSTRADE

10mm

BEAM BEARING (SAME BOTH ENDS)

CONC. PADSTONE

⑤

Job: Lampits Farm, Gloucestershire

Client: Harry Scott and Sophie Ryder

Designer: Hunt Projects

Date: Current

- The brief was to come up with alternative ideas for a large studio/sculpture workshop to be partially buried below ground in order to minimise the impact on the sensitive local landscape
- A range of options is proposed for the roof in different structural materials including timber, steel and ferrocement, the idea being to create a clear internal volume for the construction of very large pieces of sculpture
- The base slab and walls are to be in reinforced concrete with, possibly, a clerestory window around the whole perimeter
- The roof covering ideally will be seeded to blend in with the landscape
- An entrance and ramp will be formed by a cut in the surrounding ground and retaining wall

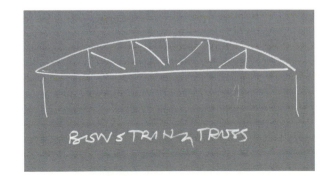

BOWSTRING TRUSS

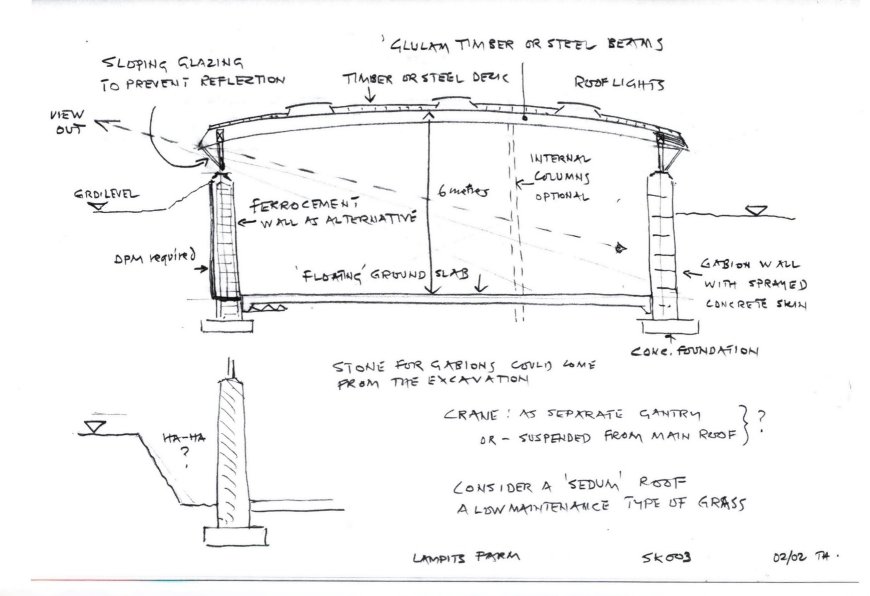

SLOPING GLAZING
TO PREVENT REFLECTION

GLULAM TIMBER OR STEEL BEAMS

TIMBER OR STEEL DECK

ROOF LIGHTS

VIEW OUT

GRD LEVEL

FERROCEMENT
WALL AS ALTERNATIVE

6 meters

INTERNAL COLUMNS OPTIONAL

DPM required

'FLOATING' GROUND SLAB

GABION WALL WITH SPRAYED CONCRETE SKIN

CONC. FOUNDATION

STONE FOR GABIONS COULD COME FROM THE EXCAVATION

HA-HA ?

CRANE: AS SEPARATE GANTRY } ?
OR - SUSPENDED FROM MAIN ROOF } ?

CONSIDER A 'SEDUM' ROOF
A LOW MAINTENANCE TYPE OF GRASS

LAMPITS FARM   SK003   02/02 TA.

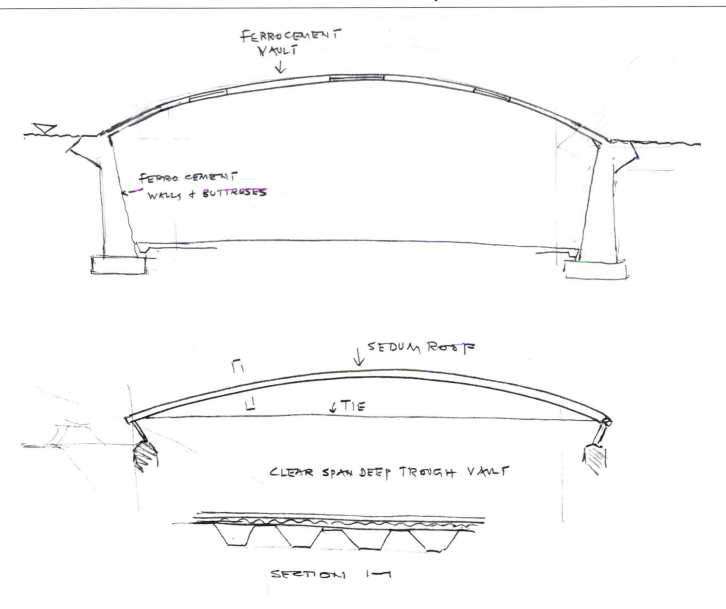

FERROCEMENT VAULT

FERRO CEMENT WALLS & BUTTRESES

SEDUM ROOF

TIE

CLEAR SPAN DEEP TROUGH VAULT

SECTION |—|

Lampits Farm, Gloucestershire

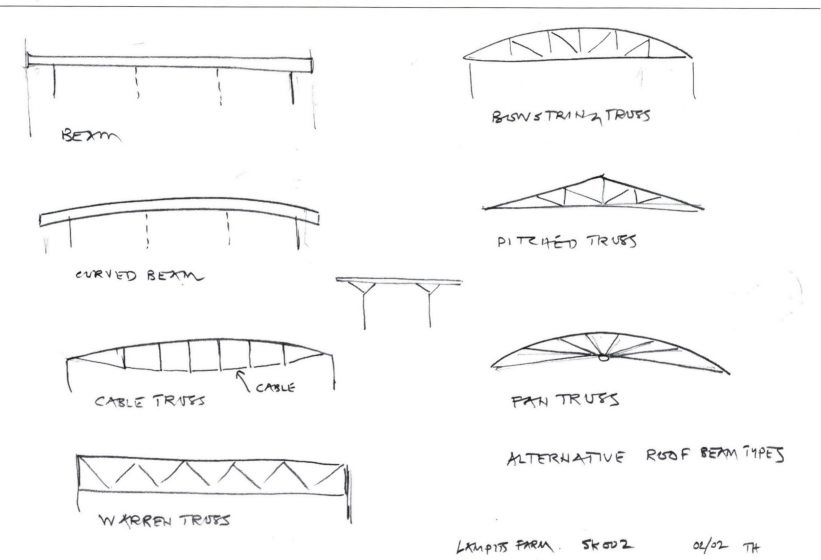

BEAM

CURVED BEAM

CABLE TRUSS
CABLE

WARREN TRUSS

BOWSTRING TRUSS

PITCHED TRUSS

FAN TRUSS

ALTERNATIVE ROOF BEAM TYPES

LAMPITS FARM. SK 002   02/02 TH

Platts Eyot Bridge

Job: Platts Eyot Bridge, Hampton

Client: Terrace Hill Properties

Designers: Anthony Hunt Associates

Date: Current

- The bridge is the only link between the island and the shore and carries pedestrians and light vehicles
- The brief was to design a replacement for the existing narrow steel suspension bridge which is sub-standard
- Four alternatives were proposed, all in steel and all keeping within the narrow constraints of the two landing points
- Bridge No. 4 was considered to be the most elegant and practical

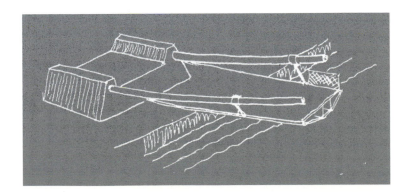

Platts Eyot Bridge, Hampton

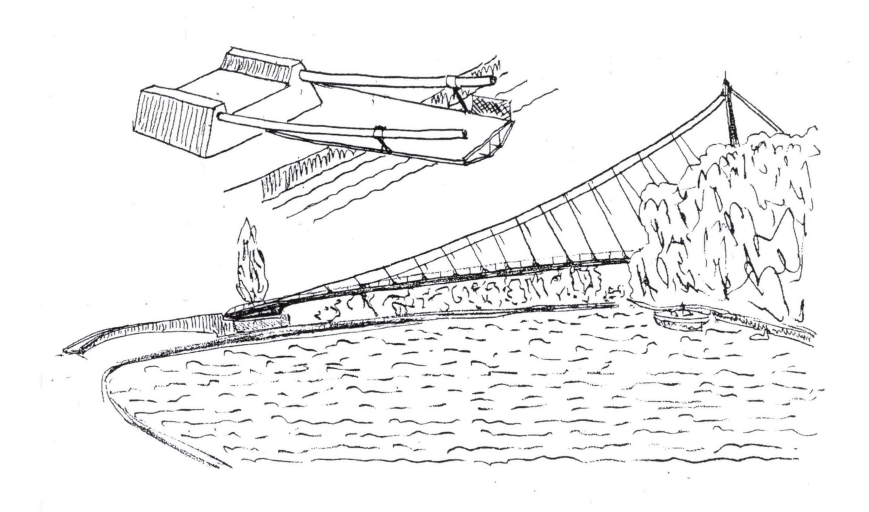

PLATTS EYOT BRIDGE SCHEME 1

FEB '00 TH

PLATTS EYOT BRIDGE SCHEME 2   FEB '00 TH

Platts Eyot Bridge, Hampton

PLATTS EYOT BRIDGE SCHEME 3

FEB '00   TH

PLATTS EYOT BRIDGE SCHEME 4

FEB '00 TH